The author, Carla Blake, pictured in her kitchen, as seen through the eyes of her grand-daughter, Andrea Blake-Böhm, age twelve.

DEDICATION

This new revised and enlarged edition of *The Irish Cookbook* is in celebration of the memory of my beloved husband Valentine, who originally came up with the idea that I should write a cookery book, and without whose inspiration, encouragement and active assistance the first edition would never have been published in 1971 – he typed the manuscript with three fingers!

It is also dedicated with love and appreciation to our daughter Rosalie, without whose determination, encouragement and sheer hard slog the large and varied collection of recipes contained in the second edition – based on my abiding interest and enjoyment of real food and good cooking, written about extensively for several national publications over the last 36 years and stashed away at random in my computer's memory – would never have been presented in the form of a manuscript acceptable to the Mercier Press!

THE
✦ IRISH ✦
COOKBOOK

CARLA BLAKE

in association with her daughters, Rosalie Byrne and Claire Blake-Böhm

MERCIER PRESS

MERCIER PRESS
Douglas Village, Cork
www.mercierpress.ie

Trade enquiries to Columba Mercier Distribution,
55a Spruce Avenue, Stillorgan Industrial Park, Blackrock, Dublin

ISBN: 978 1 85635 504 9

First published in 1971
This edition first published in 2006

Mercier Press receives financial assistance from
the Arts Council / An Chomhairle Ealaíon

Printed and Bound in Ireland by Colour Books Ltd.

CONTENTS

Acknowledgements

I would like to thank –

* Aisling Lyons at Mercier Press who was most helpful and enthusiastic about updating and enlarging The Irish Cookbook; and her colleagues, Isobel Creed and Patrick Crowley.

* My daughter Rosalie who worked like a fiend to present it in manuscript form in time to meet the deadline.

* Val and my children – Kerry, Claire, Jonny and Rosalie and their spouses and children. I have practised my recipes on them and they have helped with testing too – lovingly merciless in their criticism but always supportive; encouraging me to expand my food horizons and my journalism.

* My dear friends Heather Teap, Margaret Mellerick, Norah O'Brien and Noelle Switzer who have always been there for me, and Mike Pratt who keeps the garden going so I have time to write.

* Stephen Cadogan who's tops as an editor and meticulous in the visual presentation of my page.

* Son in law Karlheinz Blake-Böhm who keeps the peace between me and my computer, and grandson Torsten too.

* Myrtle Allen – the first and the best when it comes to putting Irish food on the map worldwide.

* Vicky Wallace, who collated hundreds of recipes in scrapbooks which would otherwise have been lost.

* The Guild of Irish Foodwriters whose members have inspired and supported me throughout my writing career – we have shared a lot of laughter together and, I hope, raised standards in the food industry while encouraging readers to roll up their sleeves and get cooking.

* Bord Bia, the Irish Food Board which does sterling work in promoting Irish food at home and abroad, enabling small producers to develop and market speciality products and keeping us in touch with new developments.

* The farmers, small holders, market gardeners and specialised food makers of Ireland who produce wonderful meat, cheese, fish, fruit and vegetables in particular; and the Country Markets and Farmers' Markets where shoppers can be confident they can find fabulous fresh produce and carefully sourced speciality and home-made foods.

PREFACE

Myrtle Allen

My husband Ivan and Carla's husband Val were at school together. Val had been brought up on a farm in Mountshannon, Co Limerick. He then became a rubber planter in Malaya (as it was known in those far off days) and Ivan became a fruit grower in Co. Cork.

When Japan invaded Malaya in 1942, Val's world fell apart. As the Japanese troops advanced, he drove bus-loads of the wives and families of planters to Singapore to leave the country. He was captured when Malaya fell and put into a concentration camp for the rest of the war.

Four and a half years later he was brought back to England, ill and emaciated like all the other repatriated Japanese prisoners of war. As he regained his strength he moved to Wales to run his brother's farm in 1947. Carla was nursing in London. In 1949 they met at an agricultural show in Wales, fell in love and got married almost immediately. Carla took to life on a farm like a duck to water.

I have long despaired that nurses rarely know anything about cooking or for that matter, cooks about nursing. This is a pity as they are so closely related in health care. After six months in Carla's tender care, the doctors pronounced that Val was actually losing weight again. Carla is highly practical, a realist, so she quickly realised that this was a cooking matter. She found an old Mrs Beeton in the house and read, cooked and tasted, and read, cooked and tasted again until she soon had Val happily fattening up again on delicious food. Thereafter she devoured cookbooks!

Val had always wanted to get back to Ireland, so in 1952 they moved to a small holding in the Knockmealdown Mountains and two years later from there to the Duke of Devonshire's fishing lodge at Careysville on the river Blackwater near Fermoy, where Val managed the farm and the fishing while Carla managed the house and the care and feeding of the guests.

At the time the Careysville stretch was the fifth best salmon fishing in the world, so lords and ladies, ambassadors, business tycoons and keen salmon anglers from

Ireland, Britain, the continent and the USA were their visitors and everything had to be just right.

This was when our husbands decided to renew their friendship so we had a get together. We met one glorious summer day for a picnic on the banks of the river, an unforgettable day for all of us and a friendship between two schoolboys became a friendship between two families.

During their time at Careysville Carla started cooking in earnest. She planned all the meals, trained several cooks because it was difficult to find experienced staff in those days and the cuisine at Careysville soon became internationally known.

She also started to write her weekly 'Countrylife' column in the *Cork Examiner* (now the *Irish Examiner*) in 1970 and her two books *The Irish Cookbook* and *The Irish Mothers Baby Book* were published by Mercier in 1971 and 1973 respectively.

When their time at Careysville ended in 1976 Val and Carla moved to a cottage-with-an-acre near the little village of Conna. Carla became a full time journalist writing regular features for a bunch of national and local newspapers including the *Irish Farmer's Journal*, the *Examiner* and *The Kerryman* and was the weekly cookery columnist with the *Irish Press* from 1976 until it closed down in 1995.

Her strength is in her common touch, her identification with all around her, her integrity and fearlessness when she knows that she is right and on firm ground.

Her articles in the *Examiner* since 1970 reflect her simplicity, intelligence and her wide knowledge and experience of food, health and everyday family and village life. She now writes about rural affairs, cooking, her grandchildren, her dogs, and the beautiful garden that she and Val made in the acre around their cottage, saving the environment and also about her travels now that she is older and has more freedom.

This revised and updated edition of *The Irish Cookbook*, first published in 1971 and on sale ever since, is the fruit of a lifetime's experience in food. It is practical and reliable like her, the first book you need and a book you will always need.

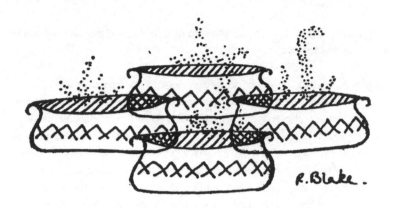

EAT AND ENJOY

I really believe that good home-cooked food made from the best of ingredients – which we have available to us here in Ireland – is one of the pleasures and blessings of life, and for many women (including me) it is one of the ways we can express our love for our partners and children.

Most importantly we can sustain their health and well-being by ensuring a balanced mixed diet based on plenty of fresh fruit and vegetables, a sufficiency of milk, cheese, yoghurt and other dairy products; meat, fish and eggs, brown bread and so on, and to get them to eat up and ask for more it is a real asset to know how to cook. And when it comes to home-cooking there's also a cosseting aspect to getting to know our offsprings' favourite dishes and making them feel important when we give them special treats on high days and feast days and on their birthdays as well.

It is also a fantastic help if the man in your life is able to cook enough to stand in for you when needed. My husband was very good at that, the proof is the recipe for Val's Mince which he created after I broke my leg and he was chief cook.

At the beginning of my cookery 'life' I didn't know any of this! Fortunately by the time we started at Careysville in 1954 I had become a good and adventurous cook because Val (who was desperately underweight and never very hungry) was put off eating the food I set before him if I told it was good for him. 'I'm not an invalid,' my darling husband said, 'I want to eat because I like what's on my plate, and not because you feel you have to feed me up,' and that certainly made me change my approach to cooking.

I continued to read cookery books avidly, extended my repertoire and adapted more elaborate recipes to fit in with the needs of the guests and the ingredients available to me, and over the years the visiting anglers greatly appreciated our 'country house' food – hams cooked on the bone, whole Careysville salmon, the best of Irish lamb and beef, roast pork with proper crackling, fish fresh from the sea, our homegrown berried fruits and vegetables including artichokes and asparagus, new-laid eggs, Irish soda bread, gorgeous puddings, Home-made cakes of every description, Home-made preserves and butter and cream in plenty.

The first edition of *The Irish Cookbook* was published by Mercier Press in 1971. This new and enlarged edition contains a lifetime's collection of my favourite recipes. It has also brought back a lot of happy memories and caused some soul-searching when I had to decide what to leave out.

Oddly enough when the word got round that I was working on it, a surprising number of people told me that 'No one is cooking any more; it's all take-aways, instant packaged food and ready-made soups to be heated in the microwave!'

Indeed, convenience foods come in very useful when needed. But if no one is cooking, who on earth is buying all those chickens lined up on supermarket shelves, the delicious Irish beef, lamb and pork from butchers as well as chain stores, and the fish fresh from the sea which is still in great demand? And why are customers flocking to Farmers Markets countrywide?

I truly believe it improves the quality of life to make the most of the here and now, taking time to do simple things like enjoying the taste of fresh Irish straw-berries in season, the first early British Queen potatoes from our gardens or the local Farmers Market; or making a little cafetière of real coffee, heating the milk and sitting down to savour the flavour and aroma instead of going on working, cup of rapidly cooling tea in hand.

It's also most refreshing to have a leisurely meal with someone you're fond of. Take time to linger over the food, enjoy being waited on, relax and be happy. Filling every idle moment with work is a waste of precious time, not the other way about, so take a shortcut now and then – and remember to smell the roses.

And if you're having friends in for a meal keep in mind that they'd prefer something very simple if needs be, rather than be confronted with a fraught hostess. You don't have to have a grand dinner party if you don't have the time or the energy. I sometimes serve something as simple as smoked salmon with salads as a main course on a summer's day, or turn a couple of shop-bought pizzas into my own creation – Poshed-up Pizza – by topping each with a layer of sliced tomatoes mixed with finely chopped garlic, followed by a plentiful scattering of grated cheese before they go into to oven – very filling, golden and bubbling on top and extra delicious. I suppose this is just another way of saying 'take time for yourself'.

Things haven't always been as easy as they are in Ireland nowadays and the tastes of long ago were hard won and cherished.

Over the years a friend of mine has given me all kinds of fascinating details about various country delicacies which have 'the taste of the old days' and bring back precious recollections of their youth to elderly people reared on farms or small holdings in the late 1930s and early 1940s, and that's why I asked her to tell me about some of them again when I started writing this book.

'Way back when my brothers and I were about seven to ten years old we'd love to cycle to meet our friends and pick wild blueberries, "hurts" we'd call them,' she began; 'There was no television then, we'd hear about everything that was happening locally and we'd be eating while we were picking, so we'd have stains round our mouths and the berries didn't all land in the empty jars we brought with us. But if we had a nice lot between us when we got home, we'd crush them with a fork, sprinkle a little sugar over and spread the mixture on bread – instant blueberry jam, you wouldn't believe how good it tasted but it wouldn't go far in a big family like ours.'

'We knew where to go to gather wild mushrooms and we cooked them in milk, they tasted much nicer than the cultivated ones nowadays, and there were plenty of blackberries in due season. We'd find wild strawberries and raspberries which were sweet on the tongue along the railway line although we'd need to be sure the train had gone. We also picked the crabs for Mother to make into well-flavoured apple jelly, and there'd sometimes be wild cherries very high up in the trees, but we were so small that it was easier to pick wild damsons in the hedges. Looking back I wouldn't have missed all that for the world – there was always something interesting on the go,' she said.

'Mother was a good manager, nothing was ever wasted in our house, and we looked forward to boiling the milk from the third milking after a cow had calved. Beestings it was called. It was very good for the new-born calves and I suppose that's why she cooked it for me and my brothers. It would curdle in the pan and we'd eat it with salt and pepper, a real treat and "very nourishing" she'd tell us. But that time a small farmer would have only about 10 or 12 cows and most of them calved quite early in the year, so we children didn't have many treats of that sort and the helpings were small but you'd never forget it – it was the taste of the old days.'

'Rhubarb was even more of treat, most cottagers and small farmers would have a long ridge of it, and once planted and spread with a load of farmyard manure every winter it lasted for twenty years although you'd have to keep it well weeded. We'd always have it stewed in a bastable hung over the kitchen fire way back in those days. Oh! The taste of it after the long dark winter, and we'd keep picking the thick red stalks right into April and sometimes May – perhaps that's why more than anything else we ate in those far off days, stewed rhubarb will always be the true taste of the old days to me,' my dear friend concluded.

I've also included a good number of traditional dishes in this book because 'the taste of the old days' is much enjoyed by returning exiles and people of a certain age here in Ireland, and they're also making comeback in various trendy guises. Besides being listed alphabetically the recipes also appear collectively in the index under Traditional foods, so are easy to locate.

One of the things that has surprised me most as I worked on this new edition is the way my tastes and my approach to cooking have changed – for instance I eat more vegetables and cook them for shorter times; and I relish a much wider variety of foods. The new everyday emphasis on fresh local quality produce and the important contribution food makes to health and happiness seem entirely good things to me.

In conclusion I'd like express my heart-felt appreciation to Stephen Cadogan, the editor of the 'Farming' section of the *Irish Examiner*, for his support and good advice over very many years; and most particularly for his kindness after my beloved husband Val died in 1993 which encouraged me to be on time for my deadlines and thus enabled me to keep on writing my column. Many of the recipes used in this book first appeared in my 'Countrylife' column during his editorship, and between his patience and encouragement and the enthusiastic feedback from 'Farming' readers I feel like I'm a member of a large gregarious family.

And finally – I'm proof that anyone who enjoys good food and can read can be a good cook! Now it's your turn, whatever your experience there is something for everyone in here – so eat and enjoy!

Carla Blake

THINGS YOU NEED TO KNOW

Healthier eating

Allow any changes you make in family meals to come naturally, adding vegetables in small helpings and phasing out fried foods gradually. Make small changes at first. Keep a quiet eye on the size of the helpings on the children's plates – it's all too easy to get into the habit of eating too much.

It's extraordinary how often people seem to think that 'healthy eating' when it comes to the family means that meals will be a sort of penance, good for you but not very nice. Let's look at the up-side of this.

We're all being urged to eat more fresh fruit, so provide gorgeous juicy oranges, apples, bananas, grapes, plums, berries or what ever else is in season as snacks through the day instead of sweets, chocolate bars, crisps and all that junk. Indeed, from the age of two or three it's a good idea to buy fruit for the children as a special treat and let them choose what they want as they grow older – I think resistance is often sparked off by the insistence that a kiwi, plum or whatever 'is good for you' and so must be eaten.

Exactly the same applies to vegetables, and there's an equally enticing choice available which can be served either raw or cooked, especially since the farmers' markets have become more widespread. So why not invest in a steamer which keeps in all the flavour as well as vitamins and minerals, show by your own enjoyment how delicious veggies are, and take the little ones shopping so they can 'help' to choose.

Overweight is an increasingly worrying problem as regards children as well as adults so try to cut down hard on the use of the frying pan, use the grill instead; get out of the habit of basting roasts with fat; and don't be lulled into thinking that using oil instead of butter or fat in cooking is healthy because, like them, oil is 100% fat.

According to the Heart Foundation it is also vital to cut down on the amount of salt we're using – it's amazing how often you see people in restaurants sprinkling salt onto their food before they've even had a taste! Nowadays when cooking for myself and the family I don't add any salt to the vegetables, anyone who wants to can add it at table. I regularly use fresh herbs and spices in the cooking which certainly helps to add flavour!

Exercise

For some, exercise is an uncomfortable word – but everyone needs to keep moving, as the advert used to say it 'prolongs active life'. Use it or lose it, a very overworked phrase, is true – evidence shows that in general people who exercise regularly are fitter both mentally and physically than those who don't. The best exercise is the one that you enjoy most – as long as it is one that allows you to work up a little bit of a sweat and increase your heart rate.

In England there is a campaign to get everyone to wear an accurate pedometer and walk 10,000 paces a day or 70,000 paces a week; this latter could be achieved by taking an extra three brisk half-hour walks each week on top of your normal daily activities.

Butter

Butter is used as an ingredient in many of the recipes because it is such an easy way of improving the taste, texture and aroma of anything from soup to savoury, but I use it more sparingly than I used to and no longer automatically put butter on helpings of cabbage, peas, beans and other cooked vegetables at table.

Eggs

It's very important to use eggs stamped with the Irish Quality Assurance mark (especially if using eggs raw as in mayonnaise or softly cooked, as in scrambled egg) because they are free from salmonella contamination.

Fresh ginger tea

Fresh ginger, obtainable in every supermarket, adds zing and flavour to everything from soups to stews, curries, stir-fries and desserts. Ginger is an excellent source of calcium, magnesium, phosphorus, and potassium, the 'cheering up' mineral. It also helps digestion, improves circulation, and speeds up convalescence after colds, 'flu and other ailments. So use it in everyday cooking as often and lavishly as possible!

Fresh Ginger Tea sweetened with honey is a wonderful pick-me-up if you're feeling cold, tired, nauseous, a bit 'down' or are suffering from menstrual cramps.

Use the edge of a teaspoon (much better than a knife) to scrape the furry skin from a 2 to 3 inch piece of ginger. Chop ginger up finely and put 1 or 2 heaped dessertspoons into a mug according to how 'hot' you want it. Top up with boiling water, and leave to infuse for about 8 minutes. Sweeten to taste with 1 to 3 teaspoons of Irish honey, add a good squeeze of lemon juice if liked, pop it into the microwave for a minute or so if necessary and drink while piping hot.

Topical Tip: Ginger holds its flavour well and I reuse the chopped ginger in the mug by adding boiling water and proceeding as above two or three times.

Gluten

Some people's digestions cannot cope with gluten. This is the protein part of wheat, barley, oats and rye. There are substitute breads and biscuits on the market but these vary greatly in terms of palatability.

If you want to thicken sauces or make white sauce without flour, you will find that arrowroot and cornflour are good substitutes. Try them both and see which you prefer – in general, 1 teaspoon of either is generally sufficient for 190 ml fluid.

Add 1 teaspoon of whichever one you are using to water, mix to a runny paste and whisk it into the stock or liquid close to the end of cooking. It will thicken almost immediately.

There are three gluten-free recipes in the baking section – Dark Chocolate Cake (page 150), Fruity Macaroons (page 161) and Sticky Coconut Macaroons (page 162).

Herbs

It seems to me that the variety of garlic available in supermarkets nowadays loses flavour in the cooking far more quickly than it used to, so when making soups, stews or casseroles I stir in the garlic, either chopped or put through a garlic press, about 5 or 10 minutes before the end of cooking time.

Rosemary adds a most enticing flavour to many dishes – include a sprig of rosemary with a leg of lamb for roasting, or chop the leaves very finely and add to soups and stews – especially good with potato soup.

Sage and thyme give a 'lift' to duck and goose stuffing in particular but use these herbs sparingly as they are surprisingly aromatic.

It's worth mentioning here that if you want to end up with a 'tasty' dish it's important to take a little taste as you go along before adding salt, pepper, or herbs, or indeed more sugar!

Measures

When measures are given in tablespoons, dessertspoons or teaspoons, this indicates level spoonfuls unless otherwise stated. The cup used for measuring is an average breakfast cup which holds 300 ml / ½ pint.

Imperial	Metric	Wet Cup	Imperial	Metric	Cups
1 teasp	5 ml	1 American teasp	¼ oz	5 g	1 teasp
¼ pint	150 ml	4 fluid oz	½ oz	10 g	2 teasps
⅓ pint	200 ml	5½ fluid oz	1 oz	25 g	5 teasps
½ pint	300 ml	1 cup	4 oz	110 g	½ cup
¾ pint	425 ml	1½ cups	6 oz	175 g	¾ cup
1 pint	600 ml	2 cups	8 oz	225 g	1 cup
			12 oz	350 g	1½ cups
			1 lb / 16 oz	450 g	2 cups

Cooking Times

Cooking times are to be used as a general guide, but as ovens differ learn to know your oven, and note whether it is quicker or slower than the given times.

Oven Temperatures

These are given as a guide to the heat required – for instance a moderately hot oven (200C / 400F / Gas mark 6) may be anything from 190C to 210C. Oven temperatures differ with the type of cooker; usually the appropriate settings will be given in the manufacturer's instruction book.

Oven	Gas mark	Centigrade	Fahrenheit
Cool oven	½	100-110C	200-225F
Slow	1	140C	275F
Very low oven	2	150C	300F
Low oven	3	170C	325F
Very moderate	4	180C	350F
Moderate	5	190C	375F
Moderately hot	6	200C	400F
Hot	7	220C	425F
Very hot	8	230-240C	450-475F
Extremely hot	9	250-290C	500-550F

This is an approximate guide, as cookers vary greatly.

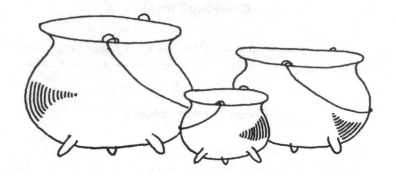

SOUPS, STARTERS AND QUICK MEALS

QUICK REAL CHICKEN STOCK

Boil up a chicken leg in 900 ml / 1½ pints water with a chopped onion and some parsley, rosemary or thyme, salt and freshly ground pepper to taste till the meat is falling off the bone. Take off heat, remove bone, skin and herb stems; then finely chop or shred chicken and return to liquid. Add to soup, gravy etc as required.

Alternatively, use Kallo Just Bouillon cubes, which I usually use as they have no artificial additives, are gluten and lactose-free and do not contain GM materials. My rule of thumb is to add 1 cube per 425 ml / ¾ pint of liquid.

CARROT SOUP

(Serves 6)

2 tbsp butter or oil (or use half-and-half)

2 medium onions

2 cups carrot cut into cubes

3 tbsp flour

2 tsp curry powder if liked

Good pinch nutmeg

900 ml / 1½ pints chicken stock (see above)

300 ml / ½ pint milk

Salt and pepper

1 dessertsp lemon juice (optional)

Plenty of chopped parsley

A dollop of crème fraiche to float on top of each serving

Gently fry the chopped onion in the butter or oil until soft, add the cubed carrot and stir-fry over medium heat for 4 minutes. Using a wooden spoon stir in the flour, curry powder and nutmeg, and when thoroughly mixed add the chicken stock and milk. Simmer gently for 20 minutes or so until the carrot is tender, liquidise in batches in the blender to ensure a smooth texture and return to the saucepan. Add salt and pepper to taste, plus a squeeze or two of lemon juice if needed to sharpen the flavour, serve hot garnished with crème fraiche and a sprinkling of chopped parsley.

CREAM OF CAULIFLOWER SOUP

(Serves 6)

1 small cauliflower
2 tsp lemon juice
900 ml / 1½ pints chicken stock or
2 stock cubes with 900 ml / 1½ pints water (see above)
25 g / 1 oz butter
1 medium sized onion
2 sticks celery
1 rounded tbsp flour
150 ml / ¼ pint milk
A pinch of nutmeg
Chopped parsley
A little crème fraiche or whipped cream (optional).

Discard the leaves, trim the cauliflower stem and make a deep criss-cross cut on the base. Place stalk end downwards in a small saucepan half-filled with boiling water, add the lemon juice (keeps the cauliflower beautifully white) and simmer with the lid on for about 12 minutes until the stem is tender when tested with a skewer. Drain and reserve 300 ml / ½ pint of the cooking liquid.

Gently fry the finely chopped onion and celery in the butter (gives a better flavour and aroma than margarine) until soft but not coloured. Sprinkle in the flour and cook gently for another 3 or 4 minutes, stirring all the time. Pour in the chicken stock and mix thoroughly, leave to simmer gently.

Reserve a cupful of cauliflower florets to be added at the finish, roughly chop the remainder and whizz up in the blender with the cooking liquid until you have a smooth puree. Add this to the contents of saucepan along with the florets, milk and a pinch of nutmeg, stir gently and taste for seasoning.

Bring the soup back to simmering point, serve immediately in warm bowls topped with a sprinkling of snipped chives and, if you like, a spoonful of crème fraiche.

LENTIL AND VEGETABLE SOUP
(Serves 6)

Very nourishing with added protein from the lentils.

- 1 large onion chopped
- 3 large carrots coarsely grated
- 2 tbsp Flora or olive oil
- 1 mug red lentils
- 1.5 litres / 2½ pints water
- 450 g / 16 oz can of tomatoes
- 1 tsp each sugar and mixed dried herbs
- 2 to 3 cloves garlic, very finely chopped
- 3 tsp freshly chopped marjoram leaves
- A little salt

Heat the oil in a large saucepan. Add the onion and carrots and stir-fry for 6 minutes. Chop the tinned tomatoes up into small pieces and add, juice and all, to the saucepan. Add the remaining ingredients except the marjoram and garlic, stir well, bring to the boil then turn down the heat and simmer for about 20 minutes with the lid on, stirring two or three times.

Check to see if the lentils have disintegrated, if not allow a few minutes longer then add the finely chopped garlic or squeeze through a garlic press and simmer for 2 or 3 more minutes – this enhances the garlic flavour.

Taste for seasoning, stir thoroughly. Ladle into hot soup bowls, sprinkle with chopped marjoram and float a dollop of crème fraiche on top of each serving (the Fuchsia brand from West Cork is my favourite).

POTATO SOUP
(Serves 6)

My version of traditional Irish potato soup, this is a top favourite in our house. It is filling, warming and comforting on a cold day, and as the saying goes 'there's eating and drinking in it'.

2 tbsp oil
4 medium onions
110 g / 4 oz streaky rashers
900 g / 2 lb floury potatoes
900 ml / 1½ pints water
2 Kallo chicken cubes
Approximately 600 ml / 1 pint milk
A good knob of butter

Heaped tsp chopped rosemary leaves added 5 minutes before the end of cooking time (failing this add ½ tsp dried mixed herbs at the start as given below) and freshly chopped parsley to garnish.

Chop the onions and streaky rashers up into small pieces, fry in the oil until a nice golden colour, add the potatoes, diced (which cook more quickly than sliced) and stir-fry over medium heat for a few minutes. Add the dried herbs if using and chicken cube cut up into small pieces and pour in the water. Simmer with the lid on for about 20 minutes or so until the potatoes are soft, stirring now and again and adding more water if needed.

When done, mash with an old-fashioned potato masher as I do, or failing this, beat with a wooden spoon until the potatoes are well broken down and free of lumps, add the chopped marjoram if available. Stir in sufficient milk to give a smooth, creamy consistency, bring back to simmering point and add seasoning to taste, keeping in mind that the rashers may have been quite salty.

Serve piping hot and garnish each bowlful with plenty of chopped parsley (an excellent source of vitamin C) and a small knob of butter.

MUSHROOM SOUP

(Serves 4 – 6)

25 g / 1 oz butter

1 small onion

225 g / 8 oz mushrooms

25 g / 1 oz flour

600 ml / 1 pint well-flavoured chicken stock (see above)

150 ml / ¼ pint milk

Salt and freshly ground black pepper

4 tbsp cream

A pinch of paprika

Fry the finely chopped onion gently in the butter until soft, add the chopped mushrooms (stems included) and cook for 5 minutes. Sprinkle in the flour and continue cooking and stirring for another 2 minutes. Gradually stir in the stock and milk, and continue to stir until it comes to the boil. Add salt and pepper to taste and simmer with the lid on for about 20 minutes. Add the cream and serve immediately if you like a chunky consistency as I do. Otherwise allow it to cool slightly, put through the blender, and reheat. A light dusting of paprika on top gives a pleasant colour contrast.

CELERY SOUP

(Serves 4 – 6)

Medium head of celery

1 large onion

2 tbsp cooking oil

2 tbsp plain flour

1 litre / 1¾ pint chicken stock (chicken cubes are fine)

A bouquet garni (sprig of parley, thyme and marjoram or a bay leaf tied together with thread) or a tsp mixed dried herbs

300 ml / ½ pint milk

Salt and freshly-ground black pepper

2 tbsp cream or a good knob of butter (optional)

Rinse the celery stalks, discard any discoloured parts and chop fairly small, saving some of the green leaves for garnish. Stir-fry gently with the finely chopped onion in the cooking oil for 2 minutes. Cover with a tight-fitting lid, turn the heat down very low and leave the vegetables to sweat without browning for 10 minutes more.

Sprinkle in the flour, stir it in and let it cook for 1 minute. Add the stock and the bouquet garni (or dried herbs) stir well and bring to the boil. Cover with the lid and let it simmer until the celery is tender but not mushy. Discard the bouquet garni and put through a blender or a sieve at this point if you prefer a smooth soup – I like mine chunky.

Return to a clean pot, add the milk (plus a little extra if the soup is too thick) and salt and pepper to taste. Reheat to simmering point, ladle into hot soup bowls, sprinkle with the finely chopped celery leaves and add a swirl of cream or a small knob of butter (if using) just before serving.

CREAM OF PARSNIP SOUP
(Serves 6)

Parsnips have a unique sweet peppery flavour – this is a lovely soup.

 1 large onion
 1 lb parsnips
 2 cloves garlic (optional)
 50 g / 2 oz butter or 25 g / 1 oz butter and 1 tbsp of sunflower oil
 1 tbsp flour
 1.2 litre / 2 pints beef or chicken stock (stock cubes are fine)
 1 tbsp curry powder
 Seasoning to taste
 Small carton cream (optional)
 Chopped chives or parsley

Peel and cut the onion and parsnip into thin slices, chop the garlic and cook very gently in the butter for about 10 minutes, stirring now and again. Sprinkle in the flour and curry powder, mix again and simmer for 3 or 4 minutes before gradually pouring in the stock, stirring as you go.

Put a lid on the saucepan and leave to simmer for about 30 to 40 minutes until the vegetables are really tender. Puree in a blender adding a little milk or water if necessary. Taste for seasoning.

(If cooking ahead, stop here and keep in the refrigerator until needed, reheat over gentle heat until the soup reaches simmering point). Add the cream if using, and serve with a scattering of fresh chopped herbs – small crisp fried bread cubes (croutons) make a pleasant, and filling accompaniment.

FISH CHOWDER
(Serves 6)

This lovely thick soup is healthy, nourishing, and filling enough for an all-in-one lunch or supper dish.

700 g / 1½ lb white fish such as cod, hake, haddock, or pollock

1 pint / 600 ml lightly salted water

450 g / 1 lb potatoes

4 streaky rashers

2 medium onions

1 or 2 cloves garlic (optional)

A little Flora or olive oil

Salt and pepper

1 pint / 600 ml milk

Chopped parsley for garnish

You can use just one kind of fish or a mixture of two or three. Divide into largish pieces, place in a saucepan with the salted water and poach for about 10 to 12 minutes over gentle heat. When done, lift the fish out on a slotted spoon, leave to cool and break up into flakes, discarding any skin or bones. Cut the potatoes into small cubes, add to the poaching liquid in the saucepan and simmer with the lid on until tender.

In the meantime fry the chopped rashers, onion and very finely chopped garlic in the oil in another pan until golden. Add to the contents of the saucepan together with the flaked fish and several grinds of black pepper. Heat the milk before adding to the chowder (this prevents curdling), stir well and bring gently back to simmering point without allowing it to boil.

Taste for seasoning, ladle into warm soup bowls, scatter chopped parsley over, and serve with brown soda cake or hot garlic bread.

CRUDITÉS WITH AIOLI
By Rosalie (Serves 4 – 6)

This is the ultimate healthy finger-food starter. Only the freshest vegetables and Quality Assured eggs should be used; what goes into it varies with the seasons.

Choose from a selection of -

Lightly steamed, just softening and then cooled – asparagus, French beans

Sliced into pencil-thick fingers – carrots, celery, fennel, sweet peppers (red, green or yellow, seeds discarded), courgettes, cucumber; also Little Gem or similar crisp lettuce, trimmed spring onions, sugar-snap peas in their pods, radishes and small florets of cauliflower

Arrange the vegetables on a large plate with the aioli in a bowl and a big bowl of tortilla chips. Garnish with herbs and allow people to help themselves.

AIOLI is a garlicky mayonnaise widely used around the Mediterranean. You can add more garlic if you like depending on the size of the cloves; but it is easy to be too enthusiastic and then the aioli will taste harsh rather than unctuous.

The secret is to add the oil very slowly, a drop at a time, till the sauce thickens and then you can speed up a bit. When all the oil has been incorporated you will have a thick fragrant dipping sauce.

2 large cloves of garlic, peeled
200 ml / ⅓ pint olive oil
2 egg yolks
A pinch of salt
3 tsp lemon juice (optional)
All the ingredients must be at room temperature.

Chop the garlic, sprinkle it with the salt and then mash it to a cream in a mortar (or on a plate / board carefully using the side of a bendy knife). Using a deep basin, beat the egg yolks with the garlic-salt mixture till smooth. Then beat in the oil as described above.

Sometimes the oil and egg mix separates, usually because the oil is being added too quickly. If this happens stop adding the oil immediately. You can often but not always rescue it by beating in another egg yolk until a smooth texture is achieved and then add the remaining oil a drop at a time.

Use up on the day you make it because it contains raw eggs.

GUACAMOLE
(Serves 6)

This is a delicious starter for a dinner party and may also be used as a healthy 'dip' with thin sticks of raw carrot, celery, and / or cucumber, small oblongs of red and green pepper. Also very good with tortilla chips.

3 ripe avocado pears

3 tsp very finely chopped onion

2 cloves garlic

1 tbsp lemon juice

1 tbsp olive oil

Salt and freshly ground black pepper

¼ tsp Worcestershire sauce

A few drops of chilli sauce if liked

Using a stainless steel knife (helps prevent browning) cut the avocados in half, discard the stones and scoop the flesh into a small bowl. Add the chopped onion and garlic (also very finely chopped) and mash well before blending in the lemon juice and oil. Add salt and pepper to taste and a little chilli sauce if you like it hot!

Chill in the refrigerator for about 30 minutes (the mixture will go brown if left too long) and spoon individual servings onto a crisp lettuce leaf, or serve as a dip with raw vegetables as above.

HOT CHEESE STRAWS

Easy to make, tasty and useful as a savoury snack when having friends in for a drink.

75 g / 3 oz grated Cheddar cheese

40 g / 1 ½ oz butter

1 egg yolk

75 g / 3 oz flour

1 dessertsp water

Salt and pepper

½ tsp mustard powder

Sift the flour, cut the butter into little squares and rub into the flour until it is like breadcrumbs. Add cheese, salt, pepper and mustard, and mix well by letting the dry mixture run through your fingers. Work in egg yolk and water until you have a smooth dough, roll out about 7 mm / ¼ inch thick on a floured board. Cut into straws about 1 ½ cm / ½ inch wide and bake in a medium oven till golden brown, about 10 minutes. Watch carefully as they brown suddenly. These can be made beforehand and reheated just before the meal.

PRUNE AND BACON SAVOURY

(Serves 6 as a starter)

12 cooked prunes

4 chicken livers

6 rashers streaky bacon

3 slices of bread

Wrap a stoned prune and a small piece of chicken liver in half a thin slice of bacon (rinds removed). Thread on a skewer and fry in butter, or bake in a hot oven until the bacon is crisp. Remove the skewer and place each 'Devil on horseback', as they are sometimes called, on a very crisp round of fried bread (cut into shape with a pastry cutter before frying).

LIVER SAUSAGE PÂTÉ

(Serves 6)

110 g / 4 oz liver sausage

110 g / 4 oz cream cheese

2 tsp port or brandy (optional)

2 tsp chopped onion

1 dessertsp thick cream

Salt and freshly ground pepper

Scrape all the liver sausage from its skin into a small bowl. Chop the onion very finely, add with all the other ingredients and mash well together. Turn into a small dish and smooth the top or shape into small pyramids on coffee saucers for individual helpings, and leave to chill.

Serve with hot toast or Toast Melba: cut the crusts from very thin slices of bread, and then cut each slice into 4 squares. Place on a wire cake rack and leave to toast in a medium oven, 195C / 375F / Gas mark 5, until very crisp and golden brown – keep watching as they burn quite suddenly! These can be kept in an airtight tin for weeks.

POTTED SALMON

(Serves 6)

Small tin of salmon

2 hard boiled eggs

50 g / 2 oz cream cheese

1 dessertsp chopped parsley

2 tsp chopped onion

Salt and pepper

1 lemon

2 tsp capers

Put the salmon and all the juice from the tin into a bowl. Flake the fish, removing the small bones and skin. Mash the eggs, add the cream cheese, capers, chopped parsley, and very finely chopped onion, salt and freshly ground black pepper, and mix well – the hand mixer is ideal. Turn into a small dish and smooth the top or shape into rounded pyramids on small individual coffee saucers. Chill and serve very cold, with wedges of lemon and thin slices of brown bread and butter.

INDIVIDUAL BAKED EGGS

1 egg

1 tbsp cream

1 tbsp chopped ham

Salt and pepper

1 small knob of butter

Individual ovenproof dish

The ingredients are for one person. You can use a tablespoon of flaked salmon (tinned or fresh) grated cheese, cooked mushrooms, or sliced tomato instead of the ham.

Butter a small ovenproof dish (called a cocotte) for each person, put in a tablespoon of chopped ham and break an egg into it. Top with a tablespoon of cream, a knob of butter and season with salt and pepper. Place the dish in a roasting pan half full of boiling water, and bake in a moderate oven (190C / 375F / Gas mark 5) for 7 – 9 minutes until the egg is set but not hard.

SCRAMBLED EGG RELISH
(Serves 6)

Served as a starter or as a savoury instead of dessert at the end of a meal, this was very popular with the salmon anglers at Careysville.

6 eggs

3 tbsp cream or milk

50 g / 2 oz butter

4 tsp Gentleman's Relish

Salt and pepper

6 squares of toast

Sprigs of parsley

Break the eggs into a bowl, add the cream or milk, salt and pepper (freshly ground is best) and beat with a fork until the yolks are well mixed with the egg whites. Melt the butter in a saucepan until just foaming, pour in the eggs and keep stirring over a moderate heat until the mixture thickens. Remove from the heat while the eggs are still soft and creamy, and spoon immediately onto hot buttered toast, lightly spread with Gentleman's relish, Garnish with sprigs of parsley.

SMOKED TROUT PÂTÉ

(Serves 4 or 5)

50 g / 2 oz softened butter

1 tbsp olive or sunflower oil

A good pinch dried tarragon or 2 tsp chopped fresh dill

225 g / 8 oz smoked trout

1 – 2 tbsp lemon juice

50 ml / 1½ fluid oz cream

Freshly ground black pepper

50 g / 2 oz finely chopped smoked salmon trimmings (optional, but delicious)

Place the butter, oil and tarragon or dill in a small bowl, and beat with a wooden spoon. Gradually beat in the smoked trout, previously skinned, boned, and finely flaked, until the mixture resembles a smooth, thick paste. Beat in the lemon juice, cream and black pepper, stir in the finely-chopped smoked salmon (if using), turn into a small glass serving dish, cover with cling film and chill in the refrigerator for at least an hour. Serve with fingers of hot crisp toast.

TUNA MAYONNAISE

By Rosalie (Serves 2 – 3)

220 g tin tuna, drained

Bunch of spring onions, chopped

50 g / 2 oz olives, chopped (optional)

2 dessertsp capers (optional)

2 tbsp finely chopped fresh parsley

2 tbsp Hellmann's Mayonnaise

Salt and freshly ground black pepper

Mix the tuna and mayonnaise in a bowl till the tuna breaks into flakes. Add the chopped onion and parsley and stir in with the capers and olives. Taste for seasoning and chill as above until needed. Serve with crisp lettuce leaves, sliced cucumber and tomato for garnish; eat with French bread or brown soda bread.

MUSHROOMS ON TOAST
(Serves 6)

Quick and easy served as a substantial starter to a light meal, this is also useful as lunch or supper dish for 4: simply divide the mushrooms between 4 slices of buttered toast, top each portion with two rashers of bacon fried and chopped and / or a poached egg and serve with a medium sized tomato, halved and grilled and placed each side of the toast.

    350 g / 12 oz button mushrooms
    50 g / 2 oz butter
    25 g / 1 oz flour
    300 ml / ½ pint milk
    Salt and pepper
    6 small squares buttered toast
    Chopped chives

Wipe the mushrooms on a damp cloth; there is no need to peel them if they are fresh. Melt the butter in a small saucepan, add the whole mushroom caps and chopped stalks and fry for 2 – 3 minutes until golden. Set 6 mushrooms aside for garnishing, sprinkle the flour over the remaining mushrooms and add the milk.

Season with salt and pepper and cook gently for another 3 – 4 minutes, stirring continuously until the sauce has become creamy. Spoon onto the squares of buttered toast, top each one with one of the reserved mushrooms and garnish with chopped chives.

FRIED SAVOURY RICE – a favourite with children
(Serves 6)

This dish uses up leftovers really well – consider adding cooked meat or fish, stew, mince, remains of roasts, capers, chopped olives, canned beans or sweetcorn – use whatever you have (but not cheese) and be creative.

350 g / 12 oz Patna rice
Oil for frying
2 large onions
Salt and pepper
225 g / 8 oz mushrooms
2 tbsp sultanas (optional)
50 g / 2 oz cooked or frozen peas
1 dessertsp chopped parsley
2 large tomatoes
6 rashers streaky bacon
Chopped garlic to taste (optional)

Cook the rice in boiling salted water for 14 minutes until soft to bite but not mushy. Strain; put under a hot tap to separate grains and drain well. To get a dry finish return the rice to the saucepan, spread in an even layer on the bottom and make small circular holes here and there with a knife blade. Place over low heat for about 5 minutes until the grains are dry and loose. Set aside for addition to the frying pan.

Heat a little oil in a saucepan, cut the rashers into pieces and fry, remove and keep hot. Slice the onions, fry till just transparent, add the mushrooms cut through caps and stalks, and fry for 2 minutes. Now add the sliced tomatoes, sultanas if using them, and cooked bacon and simmer for another 5 minutes. Add the rice, mixing it in gently with a fork, and heat until the rice is really hot. Garnish with chopped parsley.

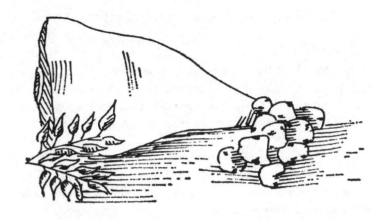

MEAT

BEEF

Beef should be dark red in colour, with a mottling of pale yellow fat through the flesh. Meat from very lean animals is liable to be dry and tough as it is the fat which keeps meat juicy and tender as it cooks. The presence of gristle suggests that the animal was old. Beef must be well hung before use – check this with your butcher.

ROAST BEEF WITH YORKSHIRE PUFFS
(Serves 6 – 7 with some left over)

Order either 2.7 – 3.2 kg / 7 – 8 lb top ribs on the bone, or 2.3 – 2.7 kg / 5 – 6 lb topside which is the meat boned and rolled, in advance from your butcher. A small joint (under 3½ lb) is not economical as it will shrink and dry out during roasting. In any case, cold roast beef is absolutely delicious.

Weigh the joint, prick the outer layer of fat with a fork and rub in a little salt to give a crisp brown finish. Place it fat side up on a wire rack in a roasting tin, on the centre shelf of your oven preheated to 220F / 425F / Gas mark 7 and roast at this heat for 20 minutes to sear the meat and seal in the juices.

Then turn down the heat to 190C / 375F / Gas mark 5 and cook for a further 15 minutes per lb on the bone or 20 minutes per lb for a rolled joint to get rare beef (in addition to the 20 minutes at high heat in each case). If you want it well done, add another 20 minutes cooking time in total. Test with a skewer, if the meat is rare, the juices will be pink, if well-done a clean golden colour – don't overcook it as it dries out.

Turn up the oven again 220C / 425F / Gas mark 7 as soon as the beef is out so it's ready for the Yorkshire puffs.

After cooking, it is important to leave the joint to rest. Place the joint on a serving dish, covered with a tent of foil, and leave it in a warm place (I put it on the rack over my gas cooker) for about 20 minutes before carving so that all the juices are reabsorbed into the centre. In the meantime you can bake Yorkshire puffs at a very high oven setting while making the gravy and finishing off the vegetables.

YORKSHIRE PUFFS

Very popular with young and old and they help to stretch the meat, so it's a good idea to make two mixes if appetites are large (in that case make extra gravy).

110 g / 4oz flour

1 large egg

300 ml / ½ pint of milk and water mixed half and half

A good pinch of salt

Sift the flour and salt into a bowl, break in the egg and add the milk and water, gradually beating as you go, until you have a smooth, thin batter. Alternatively if you have an electric mixer, beat everything together. Heat a tray of patty tins in the oven, grease generously with dripping from the roast, then pour about a tablespoon of batter into each, from a jug. Place on the shelf second from the top of a hot oven (220C / 425F / Gas mark 7) and bake for 20 to 25 minutes until all are golden, puffed-up and crisp with a lovely hollow in the middle to hold the gravy.

HORSERADISH SAUCE

You may want to enhance ready made horseradish sauce (depending on the brand) by mixing half and half with whipped cream, adding a little mustard, and a squeeze of lemon juice.

However, this is the real thing. Grate 2 tablespoons horseradish (you may have to dig it up yourself first!), mix with ½ tsp mustard, salt, pepper, ½ tsp sugar and 1 dessertsp vinegar. Stir gently into 4 tablespoons whipped cream.

GRAVY

Allow 1 tablespoon of plain flour and a crumbled Kallo beef, lamb, chicken or vegetable stock cube for every 450 ml / ¾ pint vegetable cooking water, or failing that tap water, use double quantities if needed.

Carefully drain away the fat from the corner of the roasting pan, leaving behind all the lovely dark pan juices coagulated on the bottom.

Sprinkle in the flour, add about 3 tablespoons water, and use one of those excellent little wire whisks (or failing that a wooden spoon) to smooth out any lumps, stirring and scraping to pick up all the dark flavouring fragments.

Add the remainder of the water and the crumbled stock cube, and bring to the boil over medium heat. Turn down to simmering point and continue stirring for another 3 or 4 minutes until the gravy thickens. Pour into a hot gravy boat, straining through a kitchen sieve if required, and keep warm.

If roasting a joint or bird in a bag, save the juice into a sauce pan and cook as above; starting from the point where the flour is first added but sprinkling and stirring it into the juice in the pan instead.

Steak for frying and grilling is not cheap, but there is little waste, it is quick to prepare and the flavour is delectable. Fillet steak is the choicest and most expensive cut, but to my mind the best buy is strip loin steak cut at least 2 cm / ¾ inch thick. Always ask your butcher for well hung steak. Steak may be either cooked in a pan with very little oil (see below), or grilled. Allow 175 g / 6 oz per portion.

PAN COOKED FILLET STEAK with PARSLEY BUTTER

(Allow 140 g / 5 oz per person)

1 piece of fillet steak 2 cm / ¾ inch thick

½ tsp chopped parsley per person

15 g / ½ oz butter

Salt and pepper

½ clove mashed garlic (optional)

A few drops of lemon juice

Suggested accompaniments: fried onions, mushrooms cooked in butter, grilled or raw tomatoes, leftover potatoes fried up in butter, mustard. Cook the vegetables you choose before the steak, as that must be eaten as soon as it is ready!

First prepare the parsley butter: mix a nut of butter for each person with half a teaspoon of chopped parsley and the garlic, roll into small balls, or form into small butter pats. Keep in a cool place.

Cut the surplus fat off the steak. Heat a heavy frying pan until really hot, grease by rubbing with a small piece of fat from the steak, place the steaks in the frying pan. Press down lightly with the palette knife, allow 2 minutes each side – the aim is to brown both sides to seal in the meat juices. Then lower the heat, and cook turning frequently for another 7 – 10 minutes for a medium rare steak, give about 4 minutes extra for well done. Never use a fork for turning as if the steak is pricked the juices will escape.

When the steak is done, it should be brown outside, pink and succulent inside; if a really rare steak is wanted cook over high heat for 4 – 5 minutes. I allow people to salt and pepper to taste at table.

PAN COOKED STRIP LOIN STEAK
(Allow 170 g / 6 oz per person)

Take the strip loin steak out of the refrigerator at least one hour before cooking. Trim off all excess fat, nick the edges of the steak to stop the meat curling up while cooking. Add 1 tsp olive oil to the pan. From here on the method is the same as for pan cooked fillet steak (see page 41) but allow up to 4 – 9 minutes cooking time after you have browned both sides according to preference.

HOW TO GRILL STEAK

FILLET STEAK should be placed on the wire rack in the grill pan and grilled on full heat until done to taste. Serve with salt, pepper and mustard at table.

STRIP LOIN STEAK should be prepared as given above and then grilled as per fillet steak.

STEAK AND KIDNEY PIE
(Serves 4 – 6)

1 kg / 2 lb stewing steak
1 ox kidney or 6 – 8 lambs' kidneys
1 heaped tbsp flour
450 ml / ¾ pint stock or water
1 large onion
1 tbsp oil or dripping
Salt and pepper
1 egg
225 g / ½ lb puff pastry (shop bought)

Heat the oil or dripping in a saucepan, fry the chopped onion until golden. Cut the meat into 3 cm / 1 inch cubes and the kidney into small pieces, removing the white core; (if using lambs' kidneys cut in half lengthways, remove the white core and cut each piece in half widthways), sprinkle with the flour. Add to the saucepan with the flour, stock and salt and pepper (freshly ground black pepper is best) and cover closely. Simmer gently over a low heat or in a very moderate oven 180C / 350F / Gas mark 4 for about 2 hours. Pour into a pie dish and allow to cool.

Roll the pastry until it is a little larger than required. Cut a narrow strip of pastry and lay it along the previously moistened edge of the pie dish, press it down firmly. Brush with beaten egg, place the pastry top in position, press down along the edge and trim. Make a small hole in the centre to allow steam to escape, decorate with a few pastry leaves and brush with beaten egg mixed with a pinch of salt.

Place the pie dish in a meat tin containing a little water (the steam from this will stop the pastry shrinking and falling into the dish) and bake in a moderately hot oven (200C / 400F / Gas mark 6) for about half an hour, lower the heat to very moderate (180C / 350F / Gas mark 4) and bake for 20 – 30 minutes more, cover if it is getting too brown.

Topical tip: If you put an eggcup upside down in the dish after adding the filling it helps to keep the crust up.

BOILED OX TONGUE
(Serves 6 – 7)

This is a useful cut and come again cold meat dish.

- 1 salted ox tongue
- 1 bay leaf
- 1 sprig each of parsley, rosemary and sage

Choose a tongue with a smooth skin as this will be young and tender, soak it for 3 to 4 hours in cold water, cut off excess fat. Place in a saucepan with cold water and the herbs and bring very slowly to the boil, simmer very gently for 2½ to 3½ hours, until tender. Leave to cool in the liquid. Remove it from the cooking liquid, peel off the skin (a sharp pointed knife helps), and then remove the skin and the little bones at the root of the tongue. Curve the tongue into a medium sized pudding bowl, place a small saucer that fits right into the bowl on top of the tongue and then a heavy weight; leave overnight.

Very delicious and tender; serve thinly sliced with salads, pickles and mayonnaise, combines well with cold chicken or ham. Tongue may also be eaten hot, in which case allow it to cool slightly in the water, remove skin and bones, and serve with parsley sauce (page 109) and brussels sprouts and mashed potato.

BEEF AND TOMATO STEW

Rich and heart-warming, the flavour of this stew is enhanced by the addition of paprika, a spice made from a sweet but not hot red pepper much used in Hungary.

900 g / 2 lb round steak

Oil for frying

50 g / 2 oz streaky rashers

2 large onions

1½ tbsp paprika

2 tbsp plain flour

2 tins chopped or whole tomatoes in tomato juice

1 bay leaf (optional)

1 cinnamon quill

Small carton of natural yoghurt

About 6 cloves garlic, peeled

Salt and freshly ground black pepper to taste

Cut the beef into bite-sized pieces discarding any fat. Heat a little oil in a heavy-based saucepan, add the beef pieces a few at a time and brown on all sides, transferring each batch to a large dish before adding more beef pieces to be browned; add a little more oil if needed. When all have been browned and transferred, add a little more oil and fry the chopped rashers and chopped onions for about 6 minutes stirring continuously until the onion begins to soften and turn golden.

Return the beef to the saucepan, sprinkle in the paprika and the flour and stir thoroughly before adding the tinned tomatoes, juice and all. If there's not enough liquid to come a least halfway up the meat, add a little water. Stir again, add the salt and pepper and the bay leaf if using; cover the saucepan with a piece of foil as well as the lid to keep the steam in. Simmer gently over fairly low heat for about 1½ hours or a little longer, testing if the meat is tender with a fine skewer. Stir frequently with a wooden spoon to make sure the stew is not catching on the bottom.

When the meat is done discard the bay leaf and add the peeled garlic cloves put through a garlic press, stir well and simmer for 4 or 5 minutes more — adding it at the end like this ensures that the garlic holds its flavour. Remove the saucepan from the heat, stir in the yoghurt, taste and adjust the seasoning if necessary. Serve with seasonal vegetables and mashed potatoes or fluffy white rice to mop up the thick, rich gravy.

VAL'S MINCE

(Serves 6 – 8)

Many children aren't particularly keen on vegetables but when ours were young Val discovered that if you chop the veg up really small before adding to the mince they'll eat up and ask for more. This is a very good way of disguising courgettes and other unpopular vegetables. Our grandchildren call this Granddad's Special.

2 large onions

1 tbsp sunflower or olive oil

675 g / 1½ lb lean mince

900 g / 2 lb potatoes weighed after peeling

About 2 cups water

1 beef stock cube to boost the flavour

Salt and pepper to taste

4 cupfuls or more of any combination of the following – carrot, parsnip, swede, leek, and/or celery chopped up small.

Fry the chopped onions in the oil until just turning golden. Add the mince with the water and stir over medium heat with a wooden spoon until well mixed; the mixture will be quite sloppy at this stage. Add the potatoes cut into dice or thinly sliced, followed by the chopped vegetables and the stock cube cut up small, mix well and add a little more water if needed. When the mixture has reached boiling point turn the heat down a little and leave to simmer gently with the lid on, stirring now and then to stop it 'catching' on the bottom.

Taste for seasoning after about 25 minutes, add salt and pepper and extra water if needed and continue simmering for about 15 minutes or longer until the vegetables are tender and the potato has broken down so completely that it literally melts into the mince. This gives the dish a lovely smooth texture and the authentic flavour of old-fashioned shepherd's pie which older readers may remember from their childhood.

BURGERS
(Serves 4)

A family favourite when our children were little, the unmistakeable, mouth-watering aroma while these burgers are being cooked still brings my grandchildren rushing into the kitchen asking when it will be time to eat!

450 g / 1 lb good quality lean mince

1 medium onion

1 tsp salt (or to taste)

2 slices white bread

2 tbsp milk

1 egg

1 tbsp seasoned flour

Oil for cooking

Soak the bread, crusts discarded, in the milk until soft, mash with a fork. Skin and coarsely grate the onion, or chop up very fine. Put the mince, soaked bread and onion in a bowl, sprinkle in the salt and break in the egg. The meat should be handled as little as possible, so mix very lightly and quickly together – bare hands are more effective than a spoon or fork, and the mixture won't stick so much if you wet them under the tap first!

Again working with wet hands, shape the mixture gently into 8 round flattish cakes and coat each on both sides with seasoned flour. Heat a little oil in a heavy frying pan and fry the burgers for about 3 minutes on each side. Reduce the heat and cook for about 10 minutes more, turning frequently. Serve hot with mashed potatoes, fried onions and grilled tomatoes or a green vegetable and don't forget the mustard!

They also go down well inside buttered buns, with fried onion and tomato ketchup.

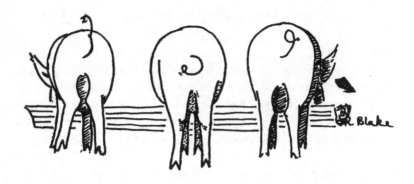

PORK

Pork should be faintly brownish pink, firm and fairly dry to the touch, with white fat and a smooth thin skin. It should be eaten fresh and must always be thoroughly cooked.

The skin of joints for roasting should be scored by the butcher. When cooked this makes the delicious crisp crackling. Pork is very rich and hard to digest, not the best choice for young children, the very old or invalids.

ROAST SHOULDER OF PORK
(Serves 6)

For some strange reason cookery books almost invariably advise using rolled shoulder of pork for roasting, and this economy joint is often sold ready boned and rolled in supermarkets. However roast pork with lots of lovely crisp crackling is a top favourite in our house, and years ago I discovered that much of the rind ends up inside the joint when the shoulder is rolled and there is no crackling.

And, worse still, the fat under-lying the rind cooks into the meat rather than melting out into the roasting pan where it can be poured away before making gravy in the usual way. So nowadays I always roast this particular joint lying flat rather than rolled. Before bringing it home, ask the assistant at the meat counter to bone the shoulder and score the skin crosswise (not length-wise) at half inch intervals with the point of a very sharp knife.

To get good crisp crackling rub a little oil and a sprinkling of salt into the scored rind before placing the boned shoulder lying flat, skin-side up in a greased roasting pan. Roast in the centre of a preheated hot oven, 425F / 220C / Gas mark 7, for 25 minutes to seal the juices in, then turn down the heat to moderate 350F / 180C / Gas mark 4 and continue roasting, allowing a total roasting time of 35 minutes for each 450 g / 1 lb plus 20 minutes extra.

If you want crisp crackling, do NOT baste at all from start to finish, and turn the heat back up to 425F / 220C / Gas mark 7 for the final 20 minutes of cooking time. Before removing from the roasting dish test with a skewer in the thickest part of the joint to make sure it is done right through – if the juice which runs out has even the faintest pinkish tinge, allow a little more time.

Place the joint on a serving dish and keep hot in the oven while you make the gravy (page 40) in the usual way. Shoulder of pork cooked flat like this is much more juicy and succulent than the much more expensive leg, and is easily carved into lovely thin slices, so it goes a long way. Serve with steamed potatoes, cabbage or other green vegetable and apple sauce – any leftover is equally delicious cold with salads the next day.

Roast Pork is often served with forcemeat and apple sauce. Small apples may be baked in their skins with the joint 30 minutes before the end of cooking time and can be used instead of apple sauce.

PORK FORCEMEAT

25 g / 1 oz butter

1 medium onion

1 teacup fresh breadcrumbs

1 egg

1 tsp chopped sage or ½ tsp dried sage

Salt and pepper

1 tbsp olive oil

A little milk

Fry the finely chopped onion in the butter over low heat until golden, mix with the breadcrumbs, sage, seasoning and the beaten egg, adding a little milk if too dry. Heat the olive oil in a small shallow tin, turn the forcemeat into it and pat out level, bake in the oven with the pork for 20 to 30 minutes until crisply browned, cut into squares to serve.

APPLE SAUCE

450 g / 1 lb cooking apples

1 tbsp sugar

25 g / 1 oz butter

1 tbsp water

Pinch of mace (optional)

Put the apples, cored and sliced into a saucepan with all the other ingredients, cover and stew slowly over low heat until soft. Beat with a fork, or a handmixer, until smooth and creamy, serve hot in a sauceboat.

BOILED BACON AND CABBAGE (TRADITIONAL)
(Serves 4 – 6)

This is a traditional dish which for many people is still almost as popular as it was in the old days – there are elderly folk in Ireland who were reared on boiled bacon and cabbage and have eaten it all their life long; and it is still their favourite meal! You need to plan ahead because the bacon needs soaking before it is cooked.

You'll often find portions of boiling bacon ready-cut for purchase in Irish supermarkets, and can choose anything from collar or shoulder bacon (thought by some to have the best texture and flavour) to the so-called 'oyster' and rasher cuts, and there's also a choice between smoked and green (unsmoked) bacon.

About 900 g – 1.3 kg / 2 to 3 lb should be enough for 4 to 6 people; make sure you have a cut which isn't too fatty. It is a good idea to buy a bit extra because cold boiled bacon comes in useful for sandwiches, and is also good served with salads, or better still more freshly cooked potatoes and cabbage the following day.

It's very important to soak the bacon before cooking for at least 3 or 4 hours or overnight as it is often over salty, and this also helps to tenderise it.

When ready to cook it remove from soaking water and place in a large saucepan, pour in cold water to come about 2 inches above the thickest part, put on the lid. Bring slowly to the boil and simmer gently for about 1 ½ to 2½ hours or more according to size and thickness.

Test with the prongs of a carving fork or a skewer at intervals to see whether it sufficiently tender. At this point remove the bacon from the cooking water and keep warm in the oven.

Cut plenty of well hearted cabbage (Greyhound is very popular when in season and so is dark green Savoy later in the year) into chunks, stem removed, put into the cooking water and raise the heat for a fast boil, cook until tender to bite. Transfer at once to a warm vegetable dish with a slotted spoon so it doesn't get over cooked. Slice the bacon onto hot plates.

Warming, filling and full of flavour it best served with floury 'poppies' steamed in their jackets – if you boil the potatoes in the same saucepan as the bacon they get very soggy. Traditionally served with Parsley Sauce – make the White Sauce (page 109) and add 2 tablespoons finely chopped parsley.

BOILED HAM, SERVED COLD (several meals)

Served cold ham is a great standby for cutting and coming again at Christmas and any other family celebration. A whole ham weighs about 9.5 kg / 21 lb. You can ask your butcher to cut it in half – choose the fillet rather than the shank end because it is better for slicing. It needs to soak for at least 36 hours in cold water, a half piece needs about 20 hours, change the water at least once.

Remove ham from water and wrap it in several layers of greaseproof paper, place in a ham kettle or large preserving pan. Cover with cold water, bring slowly to the boil and start timing when water starts to bubble gently.

Keep the heat low because the ham will start to shrink and be apt to break if boiled too rapidly. Allow the following cooking times –

　3½ hours for 3.6 kg / 8 lb
　4½ hours for 5.5 kg / 12 –13 lb
　5½ hours for 9.5 kg / 21 lb

Leave the ham to get cold in the cooking water, then lift out and drain well. The skin should come away easily, leaving a smooth surface for the finish of your choice; there are several ways to do this –

Mix 1 tablespoon of dry mustard with 2 tablespoons brown sugar and 1 table-spoon vinegar. Place the cooked ham in a roasting tin, spread with the mixture and brown in an oven at 200C / 400F / Gas mark 6 for about 20 minutes until it is a shiny chestnut colour. Leave in a cold place to set

Alternatively, score the fat of the cooked ham in a crisscross pattern, stick a clove into the centre of each square; then spread with a mixture of 3 tablespoons brown sugar and 1 tablespoon Guinness or pineapple juice. Brown in the oven for 20 minutes. Leave in a cold place to set.

DUBLIN CODDLE (TRADITIONAL)

(Serves 6)

This is a very filling dish although in the old days it was often served with freshly baked Irish soda bread.

6 thickly-cut streaky rashers

450 g / 1 lb good quality pork sausages

6 medium onions

About 900 g / 2 lb potatoes

Fresh parsley if available, otherwise a tsp of mixed dried herbs.

Remove the rinds from the rashers, cut into chunks and put into a pan of boiling water, along with the sausages. Simmer for about five minutes, drain and reserve the cooking liquid. Cut the sausages into 3 pieces, and starting and ending with layers of fairly thinly sliced potatoes, layer them in a casserole dish with the chopped onion, rashers and potatoes until all the ingredients including parsley, have been used. Skim off any fat which has risen to the top of the cooking liquid, and pour just enough into the casserole to just about reach the top layer of potatoes.

Cover with foil and a lid, and bake for about 1½ hours in a moderate over 180C / 350F / Gas mark 5 (or simmer gently, covered in the same way, on top of the cooker) until cooked through. If using the oven, remove the covering about 30 minutes before dishing up, so that the potatoes brown on top.

PORK STEAKS WITH MUSHROOMS
(Serves 6 – 7)

This is a great luxury, my own special way of cooking pork steaks, which often turn out disappointingly dry and tasteless if stuffed and roasted in the usual ways.

3 good-sized pork steaks

25 g / 1 oz butter,

1 tbsp olive oil

2 medium onions

1 heaped dessertsp flour

A wine glass of sherry (optional)

150 ml / ¼ pint chicken stock (cube is fine)

350 g / 12 oz mushrooms

2 tbsp cream

Salt and pepper to taste

Cut the pork steaks into rounds, across the grain, about 1.5 cm / ½ inch thick and discard stringy bits (there's practically no waste at all). Fry gently in the mixture of butter and oil for about five minutes, turning once, then add the finely chopped onion and cook over medium heat for another five minutes or so. Sprinkle in the flour, stirring gently to avoid lumps, pour in the sherry (if using) and the stock and bring to the boil. Lower the heat, cover the saucepan and simmer gently for about 40 minutes, until the pork is tender, adding more stock if getting too thick.

Fry the whole mushroom caps, and the finely chopped stalks, in a little extra butter, for about 4 minutes before adding to the saucepan, simmer gently for a couple of minutes, taste for seasoning, remove from heat and stir in the cream. Serve with boiled rice or fluffy mashed potato and a colourful mixture of fresh carrots cut into small cubes and boiled until tender before adding a packet of frozen peas, or green broccoli or brussels sprouts.

STIR-FRIED PORK WITH CUCUMBER
(Serves 6)

700 g / 1½ lb pork steak
4 tbsp dry sherry
4 tbsp soy sauce
1½ tbsp cornflour
1 level tbsp tomato puree
1 tsp sugar
425 ml / ¾ pint chicken stock (cube is fine)
4 tbsp oil
A large red pepper
1 medium-sized cucumber
6 scallions
Small piece fresh root ginger
1 clove of garlic
Salt and pepper

Put the pork fillets, trimmed of fat, into the freezing compartment of the refrigerator, or into the freezer, until firm but not frozen solid – this makes it easier to cut into the thin slivers required for stir frying. Marinate the pork slivers in a covered bowl with the sherry and half the soy sauce for an hour, or up to 12 hours if preparing ahead.

When ready to start cooking, mix the cornflour into a paste with the remaining soy sauce and a little of the chicken stock. Add the tomato puree, sugar and remaining stock and stir well.

Heat two tablespoons of oil in the wok or frying pan and add the red pepper (cut into thin strips, cored and deseeded) and stir-fry over a fairly high heat for about 1½ minutes – make sure the oil doesn't smoke, or discolour due to over-heating, and keep the food moving fast with a spatula, twisting and tossing from centre to sides of the wok or pan.

Add the cucumber (deseeded and cut into thin strips) and stir-fry for one minute longer, lift out with slotted spoon and set aside. Add the remaining two tablespoons oil, and when hot stir-fry the finely chopped scallions and ginger (peeled and finely chopped) over moderate heat for 2 minutes before adding the marinated pork, drained through a slotted spoon. Turn up the heat to high, stir-fry briskly for about 5 minutes until the meat is nearly cooked through.

Mix the cornflour / stock mixture with the leftover marinade and add to the pork mixture. Mix thoroughly, and allow the contents of the wok to bubble over medium heat, stirring all the time until it thickens. Then turn down the heat and leave to simmer for a few minutes more until the pork is lovely and tender – don't over-cook.

Put the strips of red pepper and cucumber back into the wok, stir well and heat right through, taste for seasoning (soy sauce is salty, so you shouldn't need much extra salt), serve at once with egg noodles, or vermicelli 'nests' which cook in less than 5 minutes.

TOAD-IN-THE-HOLE

(Serves 4 – 6)

110 g / 4 oz plain flour
Pinch salt
I egg
300 ml / ½ pint milk
450 g / I lb sausages

Prick the sausages and lay them in a greased roasting tin, about 25 × 30 cm / 10 × 12 inches in size. Put the tin in a hot oven (220C / 425F / Gas mark 7) for about 10 minutes or so, until the fat sizzles out of the sausages.

Meanwhile sift the flour and salt into a bowl, break the egg into a hollow in the centre, pour in about half the milk, and using a wooden spoon or electric mixer, mix into a smooth thick batter.

Add the remaining milk and beat well, until the mixture is light and bubbly – the air incorporated by beating will make the toad-in-the-hole rise all crisp and golden during baking.

Remove the roasting tin from the oven and drain off most of the fat; pour in the batter evenly over the sausages and bake on a shelf above the middle of the oven for about 25 to 35 minutes, cover if it is getting too brown. Serve immediately.

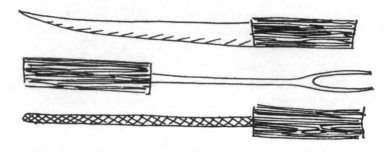

LAMB

Lamb is a pale meat and the flesh should be firm and fairly dry to the touch, the fat should be waxy white.

As a proportion of meat to bone is so high, the leg is the most economical joint for roasting. With roast lamb it is traditional to serve Mint Sauce, but Redcurrant Jelly is also a pleasant accompaniment.

ROAST LEG OF LAMB
(Serves 5 – 6)

When the family are at home or when having friends in on a special occasion you will need a whole leg of lamb weighing at least 2.2 kg / 5 lb. Rub the surface of the leg with salt and place on a handful of unpeeled garlic cloves and sprigs of fresh rosemary in a roasting dish, dot the joint here and there with butter (about 25 g / 1 oz in all) or drizzle with olive oil. Cover the roasting tin with foil tucked in around the edges. Cook in a preheated oven (200C / 400F / Gas mark 6) for first 20 minutes and, lower the oven temperature to 180C / 350F / Gas mark 4, allow 17 minutes per 450 g / 1 lb if you like it pink and juicy, or up to 20 minutes per 450 g / 1 lb or a little longer if you like it well done. Test with a skewer through the thickest part and leave to rest for at least 20 minutes before carving. Alternatively you could cook it in a smaller size Magic cooking bag than the one used for a turkey (page 79).

At Christmas this is lovely with 2 dessertspoons of redcurrant or apple jelly spread over the joint about 20 minutes before the end of cooking time, and/or stir 1 tablespoon of port into the gravy.

MINT SAUCE

2 tbsp finely chopped mint

1 tsp sugar

4 tbsp white wine vinegar

1 tsp boiling water

Pour one tsp briskly boiling water over the chopped mint to bring out the flavour and set the green colour, add the sugar and vinegar, stir until the sugar is dissolved. Mint sauce should be made about 3 to 4 hours ahead to give time to the ingredients to combine well. A side salad of sliced beetroot and raw onion cut into thin rings steeped in vinegar is an alternative to the usual mint sauce.

IRISH STEW (TRADITIONAL)

The traditional Irish stew was made of mutton, onions, potatoes and water only. Regrettably, mutton is virtually unobtainable nowadays, a great pity as roast leg of mutton with capers was a real treat in our house. I adapted the recipe at Careysville by adding carrots and seasoning and the guests loved its hearty and warming taste.

This is another plan ahead dish – stewing lamb tends to be fatty so you need to make the stew a day ahead, allow it to cool and skim the fat off before reheating.

900 g / 2 lb gigot chops

2 medium onions, chopped

8 medium carrots, each cut into 4 pieces

300 ml / ½ pint water

1 dessertsp flour

Salt and pepper

1 clove garlic (optional)

Salt and pepper

Cut the meat into pieces, removing skin, fat and bone splinters. Coat each cutlet with the flour and season with salt and pepper. Simmer the lamb with chopped onions and water for one hour, add the carrots and garlic, if using; then add a little more water if the stew is too dry and cook for a further 45 minutes.

Allow to cool overnight and the fat will rise to the top and is easily skimmed off. Being reheated like this actually improves the flavour.

Reheat thoroughly. Remove the bones as you dish up, garnish with chopped chives and parsley. Have lots of snowy mashed potato to mop up the delicious meaty gravy.

BUTTERFLIED LEG OF LAMB
(Serves 6 – 8)

This gorgeous recipe for roasting a leg of Irish lamb boned and butterflied, was devised by Bord Bia. Deliciously succulent, full of flavour, easy to cook to the exact stage of 'pinkness' you prefer, and even easier to carve into lovely even slices because the bone has been removed. This is a luxury meal for a special occasion, especially at Easter, and also very good served cold the next day. It needs to marinate for at least 12 hours before cooking

    1 leg of lamb, boned and butterflied (I asked my butcher)
    2 tbsp curry paste (optional)
    3 tbsp olive oil
    2 – 3 cloves garlic, chopped
    275 g / 10 oz tub thick Greek style yoghurt
    2 tbsp mint, chopped
    Salt and black pepper to taste

A day ahead, mix the curry paste with 2 tablespoons of the oil and the garlic, spread this over the lamb, cover and leave in the refrigerator over-night. To cook set the oven to 200C / 400F / Gas mark 6.

Heat the roasting pan on top of the cooker, spread a dessertspoon of olive oil over the surface to prevent sticking and lay the lamb out flat in the pan. When well browned turn over to brown on the other side.

Turn skin-side up, transfer to the preheated oven and roast for 45 minutes, or a little longer if preferred – it really is very delicious served pink.

Mix the yoghurt with 2 tablespoons of the finely chopped mint, the remaining oil and salt and pepper to taste, for a dressing to be served on the side.

Transfer the roasted lamb to a hot serving dish, then boil up the pan juices with a tablespoon of redcurrant jelly (optional but it gives a nice flavour) and serve with the sliced lamb. Before carving sprinkle the last tablespoon of mint over the lamb.

Serve the yoghurt dressing on the side. Also very good with butterflied lamb are baby potatoes and other root vegetables roasted at the same time with olive oil and sea salt. A real treat!

As an alternative for those who prefer lamb well done with the traditional accompaniments yet would like to add butterflied lamb to their list of favourite recipes, I made the following changes, which turned out well: omitting the curry paste, simply spread the oil and garlic marinade over the butterflied lamb, leave in the refrigerator overnight, then roast as given above, but allowing about 10 or 15 minutes longer until the juice runs clear with no pinkness left.

Serve with tangy mint sauce (see recipe above) and the vegetables of your choice to mop up plenty of gravy made in usual way with the pan juices and a Kallo Just Boullion chicken stock cube.

LAMB GRILLED ON SKEWERS (KEBABS)
(Serves 6)

450 g / 1 lb lean lamb, cut from the top of the leg,
or boneless neck fillet
3 lamb kidneys
6 rashers streaky or flank bacon
225 g / ½ lb button mushrooms
Salt and pepper
1 dessertsp finely chopped onion
2 tbsp olive oil
1 tbsp lemon juice or vinegar
6 metal skewers

Cut the lamb into 3 cm / 1 inch cubes; core the kidneys and cut each into 6 pieces, place in a small bowl with the meat, chopped onion, olive oil, lemon juice (or vinegar) and a good sprinkle of salt and freshly ground black pepper. Leave for about 2 hours or more, turning occasionally, cut each rasher into about 6 pieces.

Thread the mixture of pieces of lamb, kidney, rashers and mushrooms (if these are gently heated in a little butter first, they will not break) on the metal skewers, and place on the rack under a preheated grill.

Cook for 5 minutes each side brush with oil and grill a little longer if necessary, the lamb should be pinkish inside. Prawns, tiny tomatoes, pieces of red / green pepper or pieces of onion can also be included. Serve with rice. I always make Fresh Tomato Sauce (page 108) or Curry Dip to go with Kebabs.

CURRY DIP

1 onion
25 g / 1 oz butter
1 dessertsp good quality curry powder
2 tbsp flour
1 tbsp cream or top milk

½ tsp sugar

1 tsp lemon juice

1 clove garlic, crushed

300 ml / ½ pint stock or a chicken stock cube and water

Fry the finely chopped onion in the butter until golden. Sprinkle in the flour, sugar and curry powder, stir until blended. Add the stock, crushed garlic, lemon juice, and seasoning (not too much if you are using a stock cube as this is salty), simmer for 15 minutes, and stir in cream at the last moment.

LAMB'S LIVER AND BACON

(Serves 6)

Soft and tender done this way, but be careful not to overcook.

800 g / 1¾ lb lamb's liver

12 rashers of bacon

1 tbsp chopped chives and parsley

75 g / 3 oz butter

2 tsp lemon juice

2 tbsp flour

1 cup water or stock

Ask the butcher to slice the liver thinly. Soak the slices of liver (just covered) in milk for 20 minutes before cooking; and drain. Meanwhile, heat a little of the butter in a heavy frying pan over medium heat, fry the bacon, remove from pan and keep warm.

Dip the sliced liver in flour which has been seasoned with salt and pepper. Melt the remaining butter in the same frying pan, fry the liver gently for 2 – 3 minutes on each side. It is very good soft and faintly pink inside, but some people prefer it well done. Keep hot with the bacon.

Add a cupful of water or stock, 2 teaspoon of flour and a little salt and herbs to the pan, stir briskly and cook for about 4 minutes and pour over the lamb's liver. Don't forget the mustard!

FISH AND FOWL

Surrounded entirely by water as we are in Ireland there is a great choice of fish at reasonable prices as well as the more expensive luxuries; and fish makes a good alternative to meat as a main course.

Be sure to choose your fish carefully. If it is freshly caught the skin will be shiny and moist, the eyes bulging and bright, the backbone stiff and the flesh firm to touch. Also there will be no fishy smell – the word 'fishy' has come literally to mean 'of dubious character', so take heed! Your fishmonger will usually gut the fish and fillet it too, if you ask him. For each person buy: (a) about 225 g / ½ lb white fish like cod or hake; (b) two medium fillets of sole or plaice; (c) a whole mackerel or herring, or two if the fish are small or the appetites large.

If you have to clean it yourself, wash it under the tap, scrape gently from tail to nose with a knife to remove the scales (if it has scales), then cut the head off. Slit the underside open from the vent upwards with a sharp pointed knife or kitchen scissors, and pull out the insides. Keep the roe if there is any, it lies in sacs on either side of the backbone. Scrape all the blood away from the backbone under cold running water, and rub the black skin away from the inside with salt, as both these give a bitter taste.

FISH CAKES
(Serves 6)

450 g / 1 lb cooked white fish

2 beaten eggs

450 g / 1 lb cooked mashed potato

1 dessertsp finely chopped onion

1 dessertsp chopped parsley

Salt and pepper

For coating: a little flour, one egg and fresh white breadcrumbs

Oil or fat

Flake the fish and remove skin and bones, mix with potato, onion, parsley, seasoning and beaten egg. Divide into 6 portions, shaping each into a round flat cake. Roll in the flour, dip in beaten egg; coat all over in breadcrumbs using a palette knife to pat firmly in place. Fry until crisp, about 8 minutes on each side. Serve with tomato ketchup, green peas and chips.

SMOKED HADDOCK WITH SAUCE
(Serves 4 – 6)

In contrast with the usual poached haddock, this is a lovely filling way of serving it, keep a look out for un-dyed smoked haddock which is paler and creamier in colour with a milder taste.

900 g / 2 lb smoked haddock

50 g / 2 oz butter

50 g / 2 oz flour

600 ml / 1 pint milk

Salt and pepper

2 tomatoes

50 g / 2 oz grated Cheddar cheese

Put the fish in a saucepan with enough cold water to cover, bring to the boil and simmer until it is tender. Drain well and flake the fish, removing all skin and bones.

While the haddock is cooking make the sauce: melt the butter over a low heat, add flour and mix into a smooth paste with a wooden spoon, gradually adding the milk. Continue stirring, and boil for about 5 minutes until the sauce is smooth and of a coating consistency. Season with salt and pepper, pour over flaked haddock and put the mixture into a buttered ovenproof dish about 8 cm (3 inches) deep.

Skin and slice the tomatoes arranging them in a pattern on the top of the mixture, scatter grated cheese over and bake in a moderately hot oven 200C / 400F / Gas mark 6) until the cheese is brown and melted.

COD BAKED WITH BACON
(Serves 4 – 6)

900 g / 2 lb cod fillet
6 rashers of bacon
25 g / 1 oz butter
Lemon juice
Salt and pepper
150 ml / ¼ pint milk and water mixed
110 g / ¼ lb mushrooms
Chopped chives
Pinch of grated nutmeg

Cut the cod fillet into steaks about 4 cm / 1½ inches thick, then rub with lemon juice and salt; leave for 45 minutes until surplus liquid has drained off. Dry the steaks, season with salt and pepper and a sprinkle of nutmeg and place in a buttered fireproof dish with the chopped mushroom stalks. Dot with butter, pour over milk and water mixed, and lay rashers neatly over all.

Bake in a moderately hot oven (200C / 400F / Gas mark 6) for about 30 minutes, covering with foil if the bacon is getting over-done. Serve in the dish in which it was cooked. Garnish with mushrooms fried in butter, and chopped chives.

MACKEREL GRILLED WITH MUSTARD

1 or 2 mackerel for each person
Salt and pepper
Made mustard

Be careful to choose fresh mackerel as they 'go off' very quickly. Dry the prepared fish; cut off the heads and tails; slit from the vent to the head end, remove guts and wash away any blood. Make three slanting incisions on each side of the fish, spread about ½ teaspoon of made mustard into each incision, lay the fish on the rack in the grill pan lined with foil to save washing up, and grill for about 8 minutes each side, until the backbone protrudes from each end.

If cooking for large numbers of hungry people I usually prepare the fish with mustard and bake all together in a roasting pan for 15 minutes instead of grilling, as it's quicker (200C / 400F / Gas mark 6).

PLAICE OR SOLE WITH BUTTER AND GREEN GRAPES

(Serves 4 – 6)

8 medium fillets of plaice or sole
75 g / 3 oz butter
1 dessertsp lemon juice
110 g / 4 oz green grapes
Salt and pepper
A little flour
1 tbsp chopped parsley

Peel and pip the grapes, sprinkle with lemon juice. Wash and dry the plaice, roll in seasoned flour and fry gently in half the butter until golden brown. Lift out carefully and place in a serving dish. Clean the pan, put in the remaining butter and heat till foaming; add the chopped parsley (reserving a little for garnishing), the lemon juice and seasoning, and pour it at once over the fish. Garnish with the grapes and the remaining parsley.

OLD-FASHIONED FISH PIE
(Serves 4 – 6)

This is an all-in-one family dish, good value for money, and filling, warming and nourishing on a cold winter's day!

This recipe works well for other fish such as salmon, smoked haddock or a combination of fish. For instance 350 g / 12 oz each of smoked haddock and cod with 110 g / 4 oz cooked prawns or shrimps are delicious all layered together and extra special to serve to guests. In this case I prefer to omit the hard-boiled eggs.

> 700 g / 1½ lb cod fillet, haddock or other white fish
> 300 ml / ½ pint milk
> 25 g / 1 oz butter
> 25 g / 1 oz plain flour
> 2 tbsp chopped parsley
> A good squeeze of lemon juice
> 2 hard-boiled eggs (optional)
> Salt and pepper to taste

For the topping:

> About 700 g / 1½ lb potatoes
> ½ a cup of hot milk or more if needed
> A little salt and pepper, and a small knob of butter

First peel and cut the potatoes for the topping into evenly sized chunks and cook in the steamer, or failing this, cook in boiling salted water until soft.

Meanwhile, cut the fish into pieces, place a saucepan along with the milk, bring to the boil, then turn down the heat, cover with the lid and simmer gently for 15 minutes.

Lift out the fish and flake into smallish pieces when cool enough to handle, being careful to discard all the bones and the skin. Strain half a pint of the cooking liquid into a measuring jug.

Melt the 30 g / 1 oz butter in the cleaned pan over a gentle heat, stir in the flour and gradually add the reserved cooking liquid, stirring briskly all the time to get rid of the lumps – one of those small wire hand-held mixers is excellent for whisking!

Bring to the boil and simmer for three minutes stirring continuously until smooth and thick, add salt and pepper to taste. Draw away from the heat, fold in the chopped parsley and a small pinch of dried mixed herbs if liked along with the lemon juice, and sliced hard-boiled eggs if using, taste again for seasoning.

Turn the fish mixture into a greased ovenproof dish and top with the potatoes, previously thoroughly mashed with salt and pepper to taste and enough hot milk to give a smooth fluffy consistency.

Mark the surface into a criss-cross pattern with a fork and bake in a preheated moderately hot oven 375F / 190C / Gas mark 5 for about 20 minutes until hot right through. Place under a hot grill to get brown.

Serve with grilled tomatoes, boiled carrots or green peas and watch the family eat up and ask for more.

TROUT COOKED IN BUTTER

(Serves 4)

4 small trout
110 g / 4 oz butter
1 quartered lemon
Salt and pepper
Chopped parsley
A little flour

Dry the cleaned trout and roll them in seasoned flour. Heat three quarters of the butter in a large frying pan until hot but not brown, put in trout and remove pan to low heat. Cook the trout very gently for about 6 minutes each side, until the flesh lifts easily from the bone, place on a warm dish, and sprinkle with parsley and garnish with quartered lemon. Add the remaining butter to the pan, heat till foaming and pour over the fish.

SALMON

Freshly caught salmon is the king of all fish, it is only available in season (February through September) and very expensive. Farmed salmon can be bought all year and is less expensive.

The flesh is a delicate pink and very filling, so 170 g / 6 oz for each person is enough; though people will eat more if there is more. The head and tail and entrails are nearly one quarter of the total weight, so allow for this when buying a whole fish.

SALMON BAKED IN A PARCEL WITH HOLLANDAISE SAUCE

(Serves 4 – 6)

900g – 1.8kg / 2 – 4 lb middle cut of salmon or a small grilse (spring salmon)
Salt and pepper
Oil or melted butter for brushing
1 lemon

Clean carefully, making sure to remove the blood along the backbone, but there is no need to scale the fish, just brush it with oil or melted butter and give it a good sprinkling of salt and pepper; and lay it on a large piece of tin foil.

Bring the sides of the foil together above the fish, fold over several times to form a tent and tuck the ends in under the fish. The tent allows the salmon to cook in its own steam, keeping it deliciously moist. Bake in a moderately hot oven (200C / 400F / Gas mark 6) for 30 – 40 minutes or a little longer, test to see that the flesh lifts easily from the backbone at each end. Remove the skin carefully, leaving the delicious brown flesh beneath the skin which is full of flavour and gives a rich colour contrast.

Serve whole on a hot dish, garnish with lemon slices, sliced stuffed olives and parsley and Hollandaise Sauce (below).

HOLLANDAISE SAUCE

3 tbsp white wine vinegar

1 egg yolk and 1 whole egg

A little salt to taste

110 g / 4 oz butter, cut into small cubes

2 tsp lemon juice

This recipe is cooked in a bowl set into a saucepan containing gently simmering water; the bowl must not touch the water. The sauce needs very slow cooking and is whisked throughout cooking. You can use a double boiler if you have one. Place a bowl to cool in the fridge in case the sauce separates as it sometimes does.

Put the vinegar into the bowl (already sitting over the simmering water) and whisk the egg yolks into it until the sauce starts to thicken. Continue whisking and add one cube of butter. When it is completely absorbed into the mixture add another and another while continuing whisking, this procedure is quicker than it sounds. Once half the butter has been mixed in this way add butter cubes two at a time. When all the butter has been absorbed into the sauce, take the pan off the heat and leave the bowl sitting over water until it is time to serve it.

If the sauce separates as you are adding the butter pieces – take the cold bowl from the fridge and place an egg yolk in it, whisk till well mixed. Then continue whisking hard as you add the separated sauce very slowly to the egg yolk in the cold bowl. Once the sauce amalgamates again, set the bowl over the pan of simmering water and continue adding the butter as before; then keep warm as above.

SALMON KEDGEREE

(Serves 4 – 6)

Often served with brunch or particularly grand breakfasts, this went down very well with the salmon anglers at Careysville!

450 g / 1 lb cooked salmon

1 medium onion

85 g / 3 oz butter

225 g / 8 oz long grain rice

2 hard boiled eggs

2 tbsp chopped parsley

Fry the finely chopped onion in half the butter until golden, in a saucepan. Add the rice and pour in 600 ml / 1 pint of boiling water. Boil the rice without the lid until soft to bite (about 12–14 minutes), most of the water will have been absorbed but drain through a sieve. Melt the remaining butter in the cleaned saucepan; add in the flaked fish and the rice, lifting and mixing very gently with a fork to keep the texture light and crumbly. Chop and add the egg whites. Spoon all into a hot serving dish, sieve the hard boiled egg yolks over the mixture and scatter chopped parsley over.

FOWL

BUTTERED ROAST CHICKEN

(Serves 4 – 6)

1 roasting chicken 1.3 – 1.8 kg / 3 – 4 lb

Large knob of butter

1 slice lemon

1 sprig parsley, thyme and rosemary

1 dessertsp flour

300 ml / ½ pint stock

Salt and pepper

Boil the neck, gizzard and heart (but not the liver) with seasoning in 300 ml / ½ pint water to make the stock for gravy. Rub the butter into the skin of the chicken, sprinkle with salt; put the herbs and lemon into the bird.

Place the chicken on a metal grid in a roasting tin, pour in a cupful of water and cover with cooking foil tucked under the rim of the tin. Roast for about 1 – 1½ hours, basting 2 or 3 times, in a preheated moderately hot oven (200C / 400F / Gas mark 6). Be careful not to overcook as this dries the meat; if the leg joints move easily when lifted and the juice runs colourless when the bird is pricked with a skewer, it is ready.

Remove the chicken and keep hot, make the gravy in the roasting tin with the flour and stock, strain into a gravy boat. Fry the liver in the last of the butter, slice and use for garnishing, with sprigs of parsley. Roll cocktail sausages in ½ streaky rasher each and thread on a skewer – these are known as pigs in blankets; add to the chicken for the final 15 minutes of cooking, turning once, and serve around the bird. Equally good cold.

MY FAVOURITE STUFFING

This is my own all-kinds-of-everything stuffing which is baked separately in a shallow dish until crisp and golden. For safety reasons, stuffing is no longer cooked inside poultry.

    8 streaky rashers
    2 medium onions
    2 tbsp oil
    8 large stalks of celery plus green leafy tops
    About a third of a white sliced pan (loaf)
    A crumbled Kallo chicken cube
    2 heaped tablesp chopped fresh parsley and oregano; go easy on thyme and
    sage which are highly flavoured; or alternatively I use 1 heaped tsp mixed
    dried herbs plus 4 tbsp chopped parsley which is generally available.
    Salt and freshly ground pepper

Fry the chopped rashers and onions in the oil in a large frying pan until turning colour. Add the chopped celery stalks and leaves plus the fresh or dried herbs, crumble in the chicken stock cube and pour in half a cup of water. Continue to cook for another 10 minutes or so, stirring now and then. Meanwhile cut the bread slices (crusts and all) into small cubes and add to the mixture in the pan along with the chopped parsley. Stir and lift gently until well mixed, adding a little more oil and extra seasoning if needed.

Turn into an ovenproof dish and bake for the last 45 minutes of roasting time. Crisp up on the top shelf of the hot oven 200C / 400F / Gas mark 6 while you're making the gravy and carving the bird.

SPATCHCOCK CHICKEN

My special recipe for spatchcock roast chicken with the stuffing under the skin takes a bit of time, but it serves 4 and comes as a pleasant surprise when I have 2 or 3 friends round for a meal.

Spatchcock chicken smells good, looks good as green flecks of chopped parsley show through the golden skin, and tastes extra good as the flesh is moist and succulent having been cooked under a layer of stuffing.

1.8 kg / 4 lb chicken

For the herb stuffing:

10 slices of white bread

A good-sized onion chopped up into small pieces

A choice of fresh herbs – a bunch of parsley is essential plus the leaves stripped from a few sprigs of marjoram, snipped chives, only 2 sage leaves (the flavour is strong) and / or a sprig of rosemary – snip the leaves from the stem with sharp scissors

½ a crumbled chicken cube

A tablespoon of melted butter to bring up the flavour

I have discovered that herb stuffing whizzed up in the blender is very quick and easy to make, and gives an even consistency particularly suitable for smoothing in under the skin of the chicken.

Simply tear the bread into little pieces and whizz up in small batches in the blender adding some of the onion and fresh herbs prepared as above each time until well blended and moist with onion juice, and turn into a small bowl as you go.

Crumble the ½ stock cube in with the last batch, mix lightly together when all is done, and finally mix in the melted butter which helps to keep the chicken meat moist during cooking.

Prepare the bird: Place the chicken lying on its breast on the work surface and use a pair of kitchen scissors (or secateurs at a pinch) to cut the bird open right down the back bone. Turn the bird over on to its back; bend the ribs outwards, then with the palm of your hand press down firmly on the breast bone to flatten the carcass – the legs will automatically turn knees-inward towards the centre.

Working carefully with the fingertips, gently ease the skin away from the flesh over the whole chicken breast, thighs and legs. Insert the stuffing spoonful by spoonful, smoothing it gently into an even layer under the skin.

Place any remaining stuffing into the pouch of skin at the neck end, turn the flap under and secure with a wooden tooth pick.

Place the flat chicken on a wire grid (I use the one from my gas cooker grill pan) in a large roasting pan.

Brush the chicken skin with a little more melted butter, sprinkle lightly with salt, and cover with a tent of foil tucked in around the edges of the pan to keep the steam in.

Roast on the centre shelf of a moderately hot oven 200C / 400F / Gas mark 6 for about 25 minutes. Remove the foil and continue roasting for another 20 minutes or so until the skin is golden brown and the chicken thoroughly cooked; test with a skewer in the thickest part of the thigh and continue cooking for a little longer if the juice is even slightly pink.

Remove from the pan and keep warm in the oven while you make gravy with the pan juices in the usual way – a crumbled chicken stock cube gives excellent flavour.

The vegetables to accompany it are very simple – fluffy mashed potato, green broccoli or peas perhaps and grilled tomatoes to give a touch of colour.

Topical tip: Poultry meat (chicken, duck, turkey, goose, etc.) and pork need to be thoroughly cooked because of the risk of food poisoning. Pierce in the thickest part, usually the thigh, with a skewer. Mop the juice with a white tissue: if clear it is done. Beware of simply pricking the flesh, as it is often difficult to distinguish the colour of the juice against the golden skin.

HOT CHILLI CHICKEN STIR FRY

By Rosalie (Serves 3 – 4)

Everything is quick flash-fried at a very high temperature but it mustn't be over-cooked. Be cautious with the chilli, it is very hot; wash your hands very well after handling. You can use this recipe for beef, prawns, fish and tofu.

  2 chicken breasts or 4 chicken thighs with skin and bone removed

  Tbsp of light oil for frying

  1 medium sized onion, finely sliced

  ½ red pepper, deseeded and finely sliced

  Small tin water chestnuts (optional)

  85 g / 3 oz carrot, finely sliced

  85 g / 3 oz broccoli, cut into small florets

  85 g / 3 oz mushrooms, finely sliced

  2 – 3 cloves garlic, finely chopped

  1 inch piece fresh ginger, peeled and finely chopped

  ½ – 2 fresh chillies, finely chopped; or substitute with

  chilli sauce to taste

  Soy sauce

  Sesame oil (optional)

Thinly slice the chicken, sprinkle with a little soy sauce and set aside.

Blanch the pepper, carrots and broccoli – bring a pan of water to a rolling boil, throw them in for 3 minutes, scoop them out and plunge them straight into a bowl of cold water. When cold, strain and set aside.

Put your wok or large frying pan on to the stove and heat till just at smoking point; add the oil and swirl round the pan. Add half the ginger and stir; after a minute add the onion, then the blanched vegetables, mushrooms, water chest-nuts and garlic and fry them at the high heat until soft. Remove them to a warm plate and keep hot in the oven.

Add a little more oil to the wok, put in the chilli and remaining garlic, keeping them moving round the pan. Note that different varieties of chilli are hotter than others, and in some the seeds are intensely hot.

After 2 minutes add the sliced chicken and brown it lightly on all sides till cooked through (5 – 7 minutes), then return the vegetables to the pan and mix gently together. Remove from heat, sprinkle with a little more soy sauce, a little sesame oil and serve straight away with rice or noodles.

CURRIED CHICKEN

(Serves 3 – 4)

1 kg / 2 ¼ lb skinless chicken pieces

1 medium onion

1 tbsp cooking oil

50 g / 2 oz butter

1 tbsp sultanas

3 bacon rashers

1 dessertsp good quality curry powder

1 ½ tsp each of ground coriander, ground cumin and cayenne pepper

½ tsp each ground ginger and ground cinnamon

Up to 4 cloves garlic (optional)

½ tsp chilli sauce (optional)

1 dessertsp flour

300 ml / ½ pint stock or water

1 tbsp natural yoghurt

Remove the chicken skin and separate the leg and thigh joints. Fry them in the oil and half the butter until sealed, keep hot. Add the remaining butter to the pan, fry the grated onion and rashers cut into strips for 4 – 5 minutes; put in the crushed garlic, sultanas, spices and curry powder, fry together for a minute or two then stir in the flour.

Pour in the stock, stir and bring to the boil, add the chicken, cover closely and simmer for 20 – 25 minutes. Remove from heat, and stir in the yoghurt; the chilli sauce can be added if a hot curry is liked.

Serve with rice, chutney and two freshly sliced bananas sprinkled with lemon juice, a small bowl of natural yoghurt mixed with finely cubed cucumber and garnished with chopped parsley and two sliced hard boiled eggs.

If you don't like curry, this converts to a delicious chicken vegetable stew. Simply omit all spices, chilli sauce, sultanas and yoghurt. Instead add 3 medium carrots sliced; a small turnip and 5 sticks of celery cut in chunks; ½ green pepper sliced, 110 g / 4 oz button mushrooms and a can of chopped tomatoes.

ROAST DUCK

Roast duck is very flavourful and rich, so the portions are usually smaller than you would serve with chicken. A 1.8 kg / 4 lb duck is enough for 2 – 3 people, while a 2.7 kg / 6 lb duck is enough for 6. Award-winning Silver Hill duck from Co. Monaghan are superb and available countrywide.

Duck is a surprisingly fatty bird so prick it all over the breast, back and legs with a thin skewer (or a large darning needle), taking care not to go through to the meat, so the fat drains out during cooking.

My way of cooking the pricked duck is to place it on a rack in the roasting tin so it roasts well away from its own fat – simply pour in about 2 cups of water into the roasting tin which helps to tenderise it. Cover with foil tucked in around the edges of the roasting tin. Roast in a preheated oven at 180C / 350F / Gas mark 4 until tender, allowing 30 minutes per lb. Ovens vary, so it could be a little longer or a little shorter. About 2/3 of the way through cooking time, remove the foil to allow the duck to crisp up nicely and pour off some of the fat if the tin is filling up. It is done if the legs waggle easily when the drumstick is moved and the juice runs out clear when the thigh is pierced with a skewer. Duck is usually served with orange sauce. That, to my mind, spoils the flavour and aroma, so I serve with gravy, as given below.

When cooked, keep the duck warm while you pour all the fat from the pan. You will have a residue of duck-stock as the basis for your gravy which is made as give on page 40. Serve with mashed or boiled potatoes, brussels sprouts or broccoli, and carrots for contrast. A real treat!

ROAST GOOSE

(Serves 6 – 8)

1 young goose about 4½ kg / 10 lb dressed weight
10 g / ½ oz butter
1 dessertsp flour

Rub the skin with flour; prick the skin all over. Place on a wire rack in a roasting tin, covered with a sheet of foil. Roast in a hot oven (200C / 400F / Gas mark 6) for 30 minutes. Lower the heat to moderate (190C / 375F / Gas mark 5), allowing 20 minutes per 450 g / 1 lb cooking time, plus an extra 20 minutes. Remove the foil 45 minutes before the end of cooking time to allow the goose to brown.

As goose is so rich, do not baste until halfway through cooking time; five minutes before dishing up, crisp the skin by spooning half a cup of boiling water over.

Remove the goose from the oven and keep hot, pour off all the fat, add 1 tablespoon of flour to the pan juices and stir until browned, then add two cups of stock made from the giblets, season to taste and allow to boil for about 3 minutes before straining into a gravy boat.

Serve with double quantities of stuffing (page 72) and Apple Sauce (page 49); boiled sieved gooseberries are good too.

Duck or goose fat is very tasty for browning meat or onions before stewing.

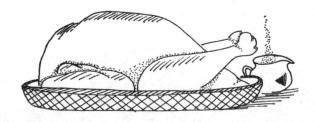

TURKEY

Buy a hen turkey if possible, as these have more meat in proportion to bone than cock birds. Frozen turkeys need 1½ to 2 days to defrost, and on the whole are drier and less flavoursome than the freshly killed ones.

ROAST TURKEY IN A BAG

Roast turkey at Christmas is still traditional in many homes, including mine. And indeed turkey is good value for money, looks magnificent when served with all the accompaniments and goes a long way so grandparents, aunts, uncles and other relations and friends who may be on their own are welcome to join the family, which is what goodwill is all about.

Fresh turkey is not available year round but there is a year round frozen supply, useful for family get-togethers and other celebrations. I was delighted when I discovered Magic Turkey Bags, manufactured in Ireland and available in supermarkets country wide, which take most of the hassle out of cooking the big bird.

Now I know from my own experience there is no longer any need for all that wrapping in greaseproof paper and / or silver foil because you can simply put your turkey into the Magic cooking bag, and it comes out of the oven very tender and succulent, beautifully browned while the juices saved in the cooking bag are perfect for making gravy.

Directions for use are given on the packet and are as follows: Place the seasoned turkey in the bag, a teaspoon of flour may be sprinkled inside if you wish. Secure the bag with the special twister tie, and cut off the extra length if the bag is too big. Puncture a few small holes in the top of the bag to allow steam to escape. The turkey must then be placed in a roasting tin at least 2 inches deep with plenty of room between the bag and the sides of the oven and put into a pre-heated very moderate oven at 170C / 325F / Gas mark 3.

The recommended cooking times at this oven setting are as follows:

    4 to 6 kg / 8 to 12 lb = 3½ to 3¾ hours
    6 to 7 kg / 12 to 15 lb = 3½ to 4¼ hours
    7½ to 9 kg / 15 to 18 lb = 4½ to 4¾ hours

Having used the Magic cooking bag many times, I find it easiest to season the turkey by rubbing a little soft butter into the skin of breast, thighs and legs, then sprinkling lightly with salt. Also, I've discovered that two handfuls of unpeeled garlic cloves put into the cooking bag about 30 minutes before the end of the cooking time add to the flavour of the turkey and the gravy made from the meat juices.

To make sure that the bird is done, use a skewer to pierce through the cooking bag into the thickest part of the thigh. If the juice is even faintly pink, go on cooking until it runs clear before removing from the oven.

When cooked remove the roasting tin from the oven, slit the bag and fold back before carefully transferring the bird to a serving dish. Cover with a tent of silver foil; leave to stand for 20 minutes for the juices to settle before carving. Meanwhile make the gravy from the turkey juices.

Accompany with bread sauce, gravy (see page 40) and stuffing baked in a separate dish (see page 72).

BREAD SAUCE

I make double quantities of this because it is so popular in our house.

300 ml / ½ pint milk
1 small onion
3 cloves
A pinch of nutmeg
50 g / 2 oz soft breadcrumbs
10 g / ½ oz butter
½ tsp salt
2 tsp cream
A pinch of pepper

Heat the milk in a small heavy based saucepan, add the whole onion with the 3 cloves stuck into it, and cook over a very low heat for about 25 minutes, with the lid at a slight angle to prevent boiling over. Stir in the breadcrumbs, salt, pepper and nutmeg; simmer gently for another 15 minutes. Discard the onion; add the butter and cream and beat well with a wire whisk. Serve hot.

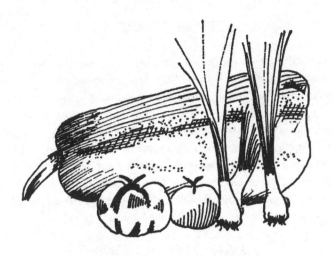

VEGETABLES – CULINARY HEROES

Asparagus and purple sprouting broccoli are my two top favourite vegetables, beautifully flavoured and a real luxury. Speaking generally vegetables are easily spoilt if they are cooked carelessly, and if you want to train up your children to eat all kinds as a matter of course, don't offer a choice of this one or that one at table. Use them fresh, grow some of your own if you can, and try to eat several servings a day.

A steamer is an essential piece of equipment for getting the best out of vegetables. They retain their vitamins, flavour and texture better than when they are boiled. Many shops sell them, choose one that has a bottom pan with a heavy base (you can use this for other cooking as well), two pan layers with holes for the steam to pass through and a tightly fitting lid. Always remember to put enough water in the base pan to ensure it doesn't boil dry and put the lid on to keep the steam in.

GLOBE ARTICHOKES

Another choice vegetable and easy to grow – a well-grown specimen forms a large dramatic "feature" in the garden. Allow one or two per person according to size. Wash, and trim the stalks, plunge into salted boiling water with a knob of butter and a little lemon juice and boil for 20 to 30 minutes according to size. They are done as soon as the leaves come away when pulled gently. Serve on hot plates with individual pots of melted butter to which is added a little salt, black pepper, and a squeeze of lemon juice. Dip the nut of flesh at the base of each leaf into the butter and savour the flavour – provide a bowl for the discarded leaves. Remove the hairy choke and eat the layer of flesh at the base with a teaspoon of melted butter. Good also with Hollandaise sauce.

JERUSALEM ARTICHOKES

Not a very widely used vegetable as yet, although the flavour is unusual and delicious and they're almost too easy to grow as they become invasive if you don't watch out! They also add to the variety of vegetables available to us and go well as an accompaniment to meat, chicken and fish dishes. Wash under the tap and remove the skin with a potato peeler, placing the artichokes into cold water with a little vinegar – this will stop them discolouring. Bring a saucepan of water to the boil, adding salt and ½ teaspoon of vinegar to each 600 ml (1 pint) – put in the artichokes and boil gently for about 20 minutes until soft. Drain well, and serve garnished with pats of butter and chopped parsley, or with creamy white sauce.

ASPARAGUS

There's nothing to equal the flavour freshly picked asparagus. It is best eaten in season. Val and I planted up an asparagus bed from plants we grew from seed in 1977. It has been well loved, looked after and weeded regularly over the years and is still very productive at the time of writing (Feb 2006).

Scrape the bottom of the stalks lightly, wash in cold water and tie in bundles of 8 to 10, with all their tips in one direction. Put into boiling salted water with a knob of butter and a squeeze of lemon juice. Boil gently for about 15 – 20 minutes until tender – check by lifting the bundle horizontally out of the water with the tines of a fork and if the tips bend down the asparagus is done. Lift out carefully or the tips may fall off, serve with melted butter to which salt and pepper is added, or with Hollandaise Sauce. If served cold, accompany with French Dressing (page 108).

AUBERGINES (EGG PLANT)

Choose shiny, medium-sized, smooth-skinned aubergines, fresh and firm with a bright green calyx at the stem end, and use them as soon as possible after purchase. Large ones tend to be spongy and tasteless.

It is a good idea to sprinkle the flesh with salt before cooking to draw out some of the juice – this removes any slight bitterness, prevents them going soggy during cooking and also stops the absorption of too much oil. Simply cut the eggplant into thick slices, sprinkle these on both sides with a little salt and leave on a tilted plate (put a matchbox under the edge on one side) for about 25 minutes while the liquid drains off. If the aubergine is to be stuffed, cut in half lengthways, score the flesh with a sharp knife, sprinkle with salt and leave cut-side-down on the tilted plate. Rinse to remove the salt and pat dry before cooking.

STUFFED AUBERGINES
(Serves 4)

2 fair-sized aubergines

1 large onion

4 large tomatoes

1 clove garlic

2 tbsp chopped parsley

A third of a Kallo stock cube dissolved in ½ cup of water

2 tbsp butter

1½ cups fresh white bread crumbs (made in the blender if you have one)

½ cup grated Cheddar cheese

Salt

Oil for frying

Wash the aubergines to remove any traces of spray, cut in half lengthways and drain off excess juice as given above. Rinse under the tap and pat dry on kitchen paper. Heat the oil in a large frying pan and fry the aubergine halves, cut side down, over gentle heat for a few minutes.

Carefully remove the slightly softened flesh, leaving skin 'shells' about ½ inch thick. Chop the flesh up into small pieces and mix with the chopped onion, chopped tomatoes, crushed garlic, finely chopped parsley and freshly-ground black pepper. Divide the mixture evenly between the four aubergine shells, place in a single layer in a large shallow ovenproof dish, pour in the stock and cover with foil. Bake in a preheated very moderate oven 180C / 350F / Gas mark 4 for about 35 minutes.

Towards the end of cooking time, fry the breadcrumbs in the melted butter, stirring all the time, until crisp and golden, sprinkle these evenly over the aubergine shells, top with grated cheese and place under a hot grill until melty and bubbly, serve immediately.

THREE DIFFERENT TYPES OF BEANS, ALL HEALTHY AND VERY GOOD TO EAT

BROAD BEANS can be eaten at two stages:

When the beans in the pod are about 1½ cm / ½ inch long, shell them and cook uncovered in boiling salted water for about 10 minutes.

Rather old pods containing large beans should not be wasted. Pod the beans, boil for 15 to 20 minutes until the skins are loose, pinch one end and squeeze the contents out. Heat in melted butter and serve garnished with chopped chives – they have a delicious nutty flavour.

FRENCH BEANS are small, smooth and crisp. They have no strings down the sides. Top and tail them as for runner beans. Cook in boiling water for about 15 minutes until just tender.

RUNNER BEANS should be eaten young and freshly picked; test by bending double, they should snap in two. Cut off both ends, and a narrow strip down each side to remove the strings, which are very tough if left on.

Cut the runner beans into small slices in a slanting direction, or better still in long thin strips from top to bottom. Steam them for 8 –12 minutes until tender.

BROCCOLI

Smells and tastes gorgeous with turkey, chicken, pork or any other roast meat. Garnish with slivers of red pepper to add a Christmas touch. Also good with sausages, grilled steak, lamb cutlets or a mixed grill, in fact very versatile.

Broccoli (Green) has thick stalks which have a delicious texture and taste, so don't discard them. Simply trim the end off the fat stalk, cut the broccoli head in half and slit the lower inch or so of the halved stalks to speed up cooking.

Steam until the stalks are just tender when pierced with a skewer or, cook in boiling water with the lid on the pan. Drain and place on a hot serving dish, sprinkle with a little salt and lots of black pepper. Better still, cut down on salt by letting each add their own.

Purple sprouting broccoli is second only to asparagus. In the garden it's a cut-and-come-again vegetable grown annually from seed. It bridges the 'hungry gap' between February and May, although it is very seldom available commercially. The purple flowering shoots should be picked every second day. The texture and flavour are delicious, preferably steamed or boiled for 8 – 15 minutes.

Optional – heat a teaspoon butter and oil, add 1 clove finely chopped garlic; cook for 1 minute then spoon over the cooked broccoli. Garnish with 1 tablespoon of sesame seeds, briefly dry roasted in a frying pan, and then sprinkle with a little soy sauce and sesame oil.

BRUSSELS SPROUTS

Choose sprouts that are small, green and firm, the large loose-leaved ones are liable to be soggy when cooked. Remove only discoloured outer leaves, wash well and make a crisscross cut on the base of each stalk to shorten the cooking times. Put into boiling salted water and cook for 10 – 12 minutes until just soft but not mushy. Drain well and serve.

CABBAGE

Cabbage is the most sadly abused vegetable of all. It is often boiled into a colour-less, flavourless, mush. Choose the crisp firm heads, if it is rather limp, freshen up by soaking in cold water for half an hour or so before cooking.

SPRING CABBAGE – remove outer coarse leaves, wash in cold water, shred with a sharp knife and steam for 8 to 10 minutes, until tender. Do not overcook. Drain well, also good with a small pinch of mace or chopped chives.

SAVOY CABBAGE is prepared in the same way, but cooked for 10 to 12 minutes.

Firm-hearted WHITE CABBAGE – remove the discoloured outer leaves and rinse under cold running water. In the case of firm tightly packed cabbage this is often all the washing needed. Cut into quarters, discard the hard centre stalk, and shred finely, cutting across the leaves; plunge into boiling water, cook for 10 to 12 minutes until tender but slightly crisp to bite.

RED CABBAGE is treated as white cabbage but cooked in a covered pan with a little water, some chopped apple, a tablespoon of vinegar and a sprinkling of sugar for 1 – 2 hours. Check regularly that there is enough water in the pan. Good as an accompaniment to roast duck or roast pork.

CARROTS

My favourite are the first of summer's crop, gathered when still quite small; served whole with a salad or other raw vegetables and aioli (page 29).

Carrots are invaluable, very versatile and available all year. Tender young carrots should be gently scraped (try using a nylon pot scraper to do this) then steamed whole if small, or cut into quarters lengthways if larger. Serve with a sprinkling of freshly chopped mint.

Older carrots should be very thinly peeled, then cut into rings, long narrow lengths or short very thin strips like match sticks. Steam and garnish with chopped parsley, chives or mint before serving. Alternatively they are lovely mashed with equal quanti-ties of cooked parsnip and my son-in-law Kevin's favourite winter vegetable dish is carrots mashed with swede turnip and a little butter – he calls it 'bashed neeps'.

COLCANNON (TRADITIONAL)

I suppose this was originally a way of using up leftover boiled potatoes and cabbage, but it is a good combination, and very warm and filling. Of course everybody used beautiful Irish butter, never margarine, in those days!

About 8 large potatoes
50 g / 2 oz butter
1 ½ cups milk
A medium sized head of cabbage
Salt and pepper

Boil or steam the potatoes until cooked. Shred the cabbage finely and boil in very little water until tender, drain well. Mash the potatoes with the hot milk, add seasoning to taste and beat in the cooked cabbage until well mixed. Serve in a hot dish, with the butter melting into a golden pool in a slight hollow in the centre, oozing across each helping as it is spooned on to the waiting plates!

CHAMP (TRADITIONAL)

Champ was made in much the same way as Colcannon using plenty of chopped scallions (spring onions) instead of cabbage – simply boil them gently in the milk until soft, add to the cooked 'poppies' and mash well, taste for seasoning and serve with butter as above and a good sprinkling of chopped parsley.

CELERIAC

Celeriac looks like a pale scruffy turnip and is useful in winter as a cooked vegetable or as a salad ingredient. It may be used chopped fairly small for flavouring soups and stews instead of celery. Or wash, peel and slice the celeriac. Put into boiling salted water with a little vinegar and cook for about 15 to 25 minutes until tender. Drain well, serve with butter and chopped chives or coat with White Sauce. Alternatively make a healthy winter salad by grating celeriac and carrots. Serve with French Dressing, see page 108.

CELERY

Coarse outer stems and leafy tops chopped into soups, stews and stuffing add great flavour. The white inner stalks are lovely eaten raw, stand them in cold water for a couple of hours to crisp up before serving, or chop into pieces to be added to salads.

COURGETTES, SQUASH, PUMPKINS AND MARROWS

I grow 'Little Gem' round squashes originally from South Africa which do wonderfully well in Irish conditions, but need space for romping around.

Pick the round green squashes when about the size of a tennis ball. Prick with a skewer in several places, boil for about 20 minutes until soft, cut in half between stem and flower ends, eat seeds and all with a little butter, salt and pepper – really, really special, often available from Farmers Markets!

The gourd family is so large that most of us will only come across a small percentage of it. Look out for their exuberant shapes and sizes in the supermarket. Try growing them – they grow visibly and store well in a cool dry place.

Butternut squash are delicious baked. After washing, pierce the skin with the point of a knife in several places; to shorten cooking time insert a skewer from top to bottom and bake it at 170C / 325F / Gas mark 3 for 45 minutes or more. Prod it with a knife and if the interior is soft it is ready to eat. Cut it open, scrape out the seeds, peel off the skin and serve it with any dish that has rich, very flavoursome gravy.

Cut into large chunks, with seeds removed, butternut squash can also be roasted with a joint of beef or lamb.

STEAMED COURGETTES – The slimmer's delight!

Courgettes are a cut-and-come again vegetable and quite expensive to buy, so it's a good idea to grow 1 or 2 courgette plants – 'grow-your-own' vegetables have a fantastic flavour and this could be a good start! Small plants grown from seed are available from garden centres and other outlets in May, keep on a sunny window sill until the beginning of June for fear of frost.

Make sure to ask for courgette Green Bush because the creeping varieties cover a lot of ground. Plant each in an old car tyre placed on well-dug soil in a sunny spot. Fill the tyre with a mixture of soil, moss peat and well rotted stable manure with a handful of slow release fertiliser, scatter a little slug bait, and the large green leaves will disguise the tyre when fully grown.

Water regularly and keep cutting the courgettes when 6 to 8 inches long – if you let them grow into marrows the supply of new ones will cease!

To cook rinse the required number of whole courgettes about 6 to 8 inches long under a tap, trim both ends and place in a steamer over a pan of fast boiling water, cover with the lid and steam for 6 –10 minutes or so until tender but not soggy when pierced with a skewer.

Alternatively you can simply cook them in boiling water. Cut in half lengthways and with a little salt and a good scattering of mixed chopped fresh herbs they're the slimmer's delight as they have a delicate flavour, are low in calories and good with meat, chicken or fish. They're also tasty with fresh tomato sauce (page 108).

ONIONS

Available all the year round, onions are used more than any other vegetable for adding savoury flavour to a great number of dishes

Onions may be baked with a roast in the oven or in a small baking tin with 1 or 2 tablespoons of cooking oil, I use extra virgin olive oil. Trim and peel one small onion per person and bake in a moderately hot oven (200C / 400F / Gas mark 6) for about 40 minutes or a little longer – ovens vary.

Cover with greaseproof paper if getting too brown. Serve each with a little salt and freshly ground black pepper

To boil onions, peel medium sized onions, put into a large saucepan of boiling salted water and cook for about 25 minutes until tender but not mushy, the time varies according to size and variety. Serve with White Sauce to which grated cheese may be added if liked.

To fry onions remove the brown skin, cut in half and cut up fairly small. Fry gently over a medium heat in oil until golden brown, stirring often to prevent scorching. Season to taste with salt and freshly ground black pepper – the classic partner to grilled steak or sausages.

PARSNIPS

Wash, cut away any discoloured parts, remove outer layer with a potato peeler, halve if small, cut into chunks if large.

Put into boiling water, and cook for about 10 to 15 minutes or until tender if tested with a skewer; they should be tender but firm. Serve garnished with chopped chives or parsley or coated with White Sauce.

Excellent also in stews along with other vegetables and delicious cooked and mashed with carrots – put the parsnips in to boil after the carrots have been cooking for about 10 minutes or so.

To roast parsnips, cut into largish chunks, blanch in boiling water for 5 minutes, pat dry and then roll in seasoned flour. Add to a roasting tin containing enough cooking oil to coat the pieces and for basting.

Roast for about 35 to 45 minutes until crisp and brown at 190C / 375F / Gas mark 5. Alternatively a most unusual way of serving boiled parsnips is to mash finely or put through the blender, and serve mixed with a little cream and pinch of mace – the sweet almost spicy parsnip flavour is magic on the palate.

PEAS

As peas lose their fresh sweet flavour very soon after being picked, choose very carefully – the pods should be firm, green and shiny, the peas inside small; if the pods are rough and whitish the peas will be hard and bitter.

Shell the peas, put into boiling water with ¼ teaspoon of sugar added for each cup of water. Drop in a sprig of fresh mint and cook for about 8 minutes, drain and serve.

Frozen peas are a very good buy year round because they are so quickly frozen that the vitamins are captured. My favourite ones are petit pois.

Peas with young carrots make a delectable and colourful combination in spring. Scrape small young carrots, cut into dice and put into just enough boiling water to cover. Cook with the lid on for 10 minutes, add the shelled peas and boil again for 5 to 8 minutes, adding a little more water if necessary. Drain and serve garnished with freshly chopped mint.

POTATOES

Make the best of Irish-grown NEW POTATOES when they become available around the beginning of June at Farmers Markets and other outlets. They must be cooked in a steamer because if boiled they tend to disintegrate and get mushy.

Flavour and texture are best when freshly harvested so test to make sure the thin papery skin rubs off easily and buy just enough for immediate use, and (unless you intend to bake them) choose the smaller ones.

I find that the best way of cooking freshly dug new potatoes is in a steamer. They are done when still firm but tender when pierced with a thin skewer. Serve with a little butter and fresh mint.

They're also delicious in potato salad – steam as above then slice thickly, mix with plenty of finely chopped onion and fresh herbs (parsley, thyme or oregano) and toss while still warm in an oil and vinegar dressing or your favourite brand of mayonnaise.

Left-over boiled potatoes: fry a little onion in oil until golden, add the peeled and sliced potatoes, salt and pepper and cook until hot right through. A little chopped ham or bacon adds flavour.

MAIN-CROP POTATOES can be baked in their jackets. Simply scrub as many even-sized, fairly large potatoes as needed, prick all over with a fork, rub with butter if a soft skin is preferred – in our family we like them best baked just as they are for a crisper finish.

Lay on a baking tray so that they're not touching and bake in a moderately hot oven at 200C / 400F / Gas mark 6 for 45 minutes to an hour, according to size. Halfway through cooking time, prick each once or twice with a skewer to let the steam out (this makes them more floury); they are ready when they feel soft when gently squeezed.

If you want to use baked potatoes as a light meal cut in half length ways and top with cottage cheese previously mashed with crushed garlic, chopped parsley, 2 teaspoons of chutney, salt and freshly ground pepper, or the fillings given under the Milly-Molly-Mandy potatoes below and be sure to eat the skins as well to get the full benefit of all those vitamins and minerals.

MILLY-MOLLY-MANDY POTATOES

These were a great favourite in our family when I was a little girl, and proved just as popular as a supper dish with my own children, in due course – also marvellous for tempting the appetite of a youngster who is just recovering from any kind of illness, especially if the smooth fluffy filling is eaten with a teaspoon. Much liked by grown-ups too, they're so warming and filling.

Bake the required number of potatoes, cut off the top, scoop out the contents without damaging the outer skin, and put into a warmed bowl.

Add a good dollop of butter (not margarine), salt and freshly-ground black pepper, and enough hot milk to make a light smooth puree when whizzed up with the hand electric mixer – it takes more milk than you'd expect, so keep adding more until the consistency is just right.

Taste for seasoning, spoon the puree back into the skins, rounding the tops, and place standing close together on an ovenproof dish, put back into a hot oven until the tops are slightly browned, and the filling is thoroughly reheated.

Alternatively, cut the baked potatoes in half across the length, whizz up the potato mixture as given above, and fill back into the halved skins, rounding the top, reheat in the oven until nicely browned on top, and serve as an accompaniment to a hearty stew.

BOXTY (TRADITIONAL)

450 g / 1 lb potatoes

110 g / 4 oz flour

½ tsp baking powder

1 tsp salt

1 egg

A little milk

Peel the potatoes; boil half of them until soft, drain and mash them. While this is going on grate the remaining raw potatoes.

Mix the mashed potato, raw potato, sifted flour, salt and baking powder into a soft dough with the egg and a little milk if needed.

Drop dessertspoonfuls of the mix on to a hot greased griddle or heavy iron pan and cook over a medium heat until nicely browned underneath, turn and cook through on the other side. Serve hot with lots of butter.

CHEESY LYONNAISE POTATOES

(Serves 4)

450 g / 1 lb onions

900 g / 2 lb potatoes

About 2 tbsp sunflower oil,

2 cloves of garlic

A good knob of butter

110 g / 4 oz grated Irish Cheddar cheese.

Slice the onions fairly thinly and fry in batches with the very finely chopped garlic in the oil until beginning to change colour. Meanwhile peel and slice the potatoes, also fairly thinly. Arrange the potatoes and onions in alternate layers in a well buttered oven-proof dish (1.2 litre / 2 pint sized), starting and finishing with the potato and adding a light dusting of salt with a few grinds of black pepper between the layers.

Dot the surface with the slivers of butter, cover with a piece of butter-paper and bake in a moderate preheated oven 190C / 375F / Gas mark 5 for about 1 ¼ hours. Remove the butter paper, cover the top with an even layer of grated cheese and bake for a further 10 minutes or so until the potato is completely soft when priced with a skewer. Serve hot, all golden and melty.

CRISPY ROAST POTATOES

I learnt from my brother Christopher in South Africa, that it's a good idea to invest in a miniature worktop electric oven which can be preheated to 200C / 400F /Gas mark 6 for roasting potatoes (or cooking Yorkshire puffs) when the cooker oven-space is full, as often happens when you're roasting a joint of lamb or beef.

Small potatoes tend to dry out during roasting, so select the required number of medium-sized old potatoes, or failing this use slightly larger old potatoes cut into halves lengthways.

Peel the potatoes, cut in half lengthways if too large, and place in a saucepan. Cover with cold water, bring to boiling point and continue to boil for 5 minutes. Remove from the water, pat dry with kitchen paper towels and score the surface of the potatoes with the tines of a fork, sprinkle lightly with a little salt, then proceed as follows:

• Either arrange the potatoes around the joint for the last hour or so of roasting time, baste well and return to the oven, repeat the basting 3 or 4 times. They will be done when golden and crisp outside and tender when pierced with a skewer,

• Alternatively I find you get a crisper finish if you preheat the stand-by oven to 200C / 400 F / Gas mark 6, pour sufficient sunflower or olive oil to be used for basting into a roasting tin large enough to hold the potatoes, heat in the oven. Add the potatoes, turn over and over until coated in oil and roast for 40 to 50 minutes, basting 2 or 3 times until golden and crusty; test for doneness with skewer.

Drain on kitchen paper, and put into a serving dish which can be kept hot in the standby oven. Serve as soon as possible before the crispness is lost!

SWEET POTATOES

This is an unfamiliar vegetable to many of us, but it's always worth having a taste to see whether you'll like it or not, so start with just one!

Sweet potatoes can be roasted, mashed and added to stews as well but they need a shorter cooking time than the more usual spuds.

Although you can add all sorts of extra ingredients (brown sugar, cinnamon, orange juice, melted butter, orange liqueur, and / or a dash of whiskey), sweet potatoes baked in their jackets in a moderate oven (190C / 375F / Gas mark 5) for about 30 to 50 minutes according to size are sweet enough for my taste.

Simply scrub the required number of sweet potatoes under the tap, prick them all over with a skewer, and place in the oven, set to the temperature above.

Check every now and then, squeezing gently in a tea towel as they're quite hot to handle, and when there's enough 'give', start testing them with a skewer to see if they're ready.

If so, cut in half, the flesh is orange / red and very soft and moist. Sprinkle on a little cinnamon if liked and add one or two of the ingredients above according to taste, bearing in mind that flavour is already quite sweet.

Eat with brown bread and butter, or as a vegetable with roast pork, pork chops, lamb cutlets or curry.

SPINACH

A good easy-to-grow green vegetable, the summer leaf spinach is sown between mid March, April or May, and the picking time is from June to December – the leaves are tender even after it has gone to seed.

Perpetual spinach (Swiss Chard) which has a wide white mid-rib (which can be cut into short lengths and cooked in boiling water until tender) and fleshier leaves is sown between a April, May and June and pickable from about August until the following March or April. Often available from the Country Markets and / or the Farmers Markets.

Spinach cooks down (shrinks) in the most amazing way. Allow about 1.2 kg / 2½ lb for 4 people. Wash well in cold water, tear out the centre mid rib, put the green leaves into a large saucepan – the water on the leaves is sufficient – and cook with a lid on for 10 –12 minutes.

Drain well, pressing out as much water as possible, chop very finely with a sharp knife or put through the blender. Elegant served with a thin slice of ham just big enough to cover each portion, topped with 1 or 2 soft yolk poached eggs and a dollop of Hollandaise Sauce (page 69) – this is known as Eggs Benedict!

SWEDE TURNIPS

Swede turnips are good keepers after harvesting, and are available in the "hungry gap" when it comes to homegrown fresh vegetables during the winter and early spring. Cut into 1 to 2 inch cubes, steam or cook in boiling water until tender, good served with parsley sauce. Also makes a nice change boiled with bacon in place of the usual cabbage. Cut into large chunks and cook and serve as for parsnips.

TOMATOES

Tomatoes, like mushrooms and onions, are used in many savoury dishes. Choose those which are shiny, firm and well coloured, avoid overripe ones as they go bad very quickly. Unevenly shaped tomatoes often have excellent flavour, as do the tiny ones which are often available when home grown tomatoes are in season. To peel tomatoes leave for 20 seconds in a bowl of boiling water then pour cold water over – the skin will strip off easily.

ONION AND TOMATO BAKE
(Serves 6)

An old style accompaniment to roast chicken or lamb, this savoury vegetable dish is a useful alternative to stuffing and also goes well with grilled chops and sausage.

4 or 5 medium tomatoes, skinned and sliced

2 large onions finely chopped

1½ cups of breadcrumbs mixed with 25 g / 1 oz melted butter

1 tbsp of freshly chopped mixed or 1 tsp of dried herbs

Salt and ground black pepper to taste

Arrange the tomato, onion, herbs and breadcrumbs in layers in a small oven-proof dish seasoning lightly as you go and ending with a layer of breadcrumbs. Bake in a preheated oven 180C / 350F / Gas mark 4 for about 45 minutes until the top is nicely browned and the onion tender when tested with a skewer.

GRILLED TOMATOES

Cut in half, place under grill cut side up, and grill for 4-5 minutes turning once.

WHITE TURNIPS

Choose small young turnips. Scrub clean, discard first slice from leaf and root end, cut in half if large and cook in simmering water for about 10–15 minutes until soft when tested with a skewer. Best raw in salads sliced very thinly.

ROASTED VEGETABLES

A selection of:

> 2.5 to 5 cm / 1½ to 2 inch chunks of carrot, parsnip, peeled potato, onion quartered, butternut squash or pumpkin and new potatoes, unpeeled garlic cloves.
> Olive oil for cooking
> Salt and pepper to taste.

Wash and prepare the vegetables. Warm a roasting pan and put in just enough oil to cover the bottom of the pan.

Put all the vegetable chunks in and swish them around so that they are glazed with the oil. Sprinkle with salt. Put into an oven at 200C / 400F / Gas mark 6 for about ¾ hour.

Turn them over after about 30 minutes and continue roasting till they are cooked – salt and pepper to taste. Serve hot with roast beef, lamb or chicken.

VEGETABLE STIR-FRY

Use any vegetables in season. Choose from any of the following: sliced onion, celery, runner and / or French beans, carrot, turnip and / or parsnip, mushrooms, sweet peppers (red, green or yellow, seeds discarded), leeks or courgettes, all of which can be thinly sliced.

Also small florets of cauliflower and green or purple-sprouting broccoli, and bean sprouts, sliced bamboo shoots and / or tinned baby sweetcorn to add an exotic touch.

Prepare the chosen vegetables just before you intend to start cooking, separating them into bowls according to length of cooking time needed – this way you can add them to the wok / pan at intervals of a few minutes.

Heat the oil over a high flame, allowing 1 tablespoon of oil in a wok, 3 table-spoons in a large frying pan. Then fry the onions and / or leeks for a couple of minutes before adding strips of parsnip, turnip and / or carrot, which take the longest to cook.

These are followed in about 4 minutes by a mixture of any of the remaining vegetables listed above – garlic and bean sprouts, either fresh or tinned go in last.

Lift and mix with two forks (or even better, use light wooden utensils) all through the cooking time, adding a little extra oil if needed, until the vegetables are sufficiently cooked yet still firm and crunchy to bite. Total cooking time is about 8 to 12 minutes, and after experimenting two or three times you'll discover the textures and combinations you and the family like best.

Add extra flavour with a light touch – sesame oil adds a lovely nutty taste but should be added once cooking stops; soy sauce adds a rich salty flavour and / or add hot chilli sauce for zest.

If you want, you can add leftover cooked chicken, cold meat, ham cut up fairly small towards the end of cooking time.

SALADS

Salads should be kept cool and covered until they are used. It is best to serve them as quickly as possible after they have been prepared.

Use only young, crisp and freshly gathered ingredients, be sure that all the moisture is removed after washing lettuce, which usually forms the basis of most salads. I use a salad spinner for this. Fresh young spinach, and nasturtium leaves and flowers may be also used in salads.

URSULA'S SALAD DRESSING

I asked my daughter-in-law Ursula (married to my son Kerry) for her salad dressing as their three children – twins Jonathan and Catriona, now age 9, and Alex, age 8 – ask for second helpings of salad, lettuce in particular.

    6 tablespoons olive oil
    3 tablespoons balsamic vinegar
    A scant teasp sugar
    2 grinds of pepper
    A good tablespoon chopped herbs – marjoram, oregano, chives and parsley
    (or a teaspoon of mixed dried herbs if the fresh ones are unavailable)
    ½ teaspoon finely chopped onion – optional.

Put all together into a small jar with a lid. Shake well. Leave for a day or so in the refrigerator for the flavours to marry and shake well again each time you use it.

As I've seen for myself the children like the herby, spicy, slightly sweet flavour especially with shredded lettuce, they eat up and ask for more and it's equally popular with adults.

TOMATO MOZZARELLA SALAD

By Rosalie

    175 g / 6 oz mozzarella cheese, sliced (buffalo is nicest)
    275 g / 10 oz firm ripe tomatoes, sliced
    Handful of fresh basil, chopped – use parsley if not available
    1 large clove garlic, finely chopped
    75 g / 3 oz black olives (optional)
    5 tbsp extra virgin olive oil
    Freshly ground black pepper to taste

Layer the cheese and tomatoes together in a bowl. Sprinkle on the olives, herbs and garlic; drizzle on the olive oil and allow to rest in a cool place for an hour while the flavours combine. Grind on the black pepper just before serving. Eat with fresh rolls or baguettes, preferably in a sunny garden.

COLESLAW

(Enough for 6-8 servings)

About 4 cups finely shredded white cabbage

6 stalks chopped celery

1 large finely chopped onion

4 large grated carrots

Juice of ½ lemon

2 – 3 tbsp of Hellmann's mayonnaise or a dressing made from 2 tbsp olive oil and 140 g / 5 oz Greek-style yoghurt mixed well and seasoned to taste with salt and freshly – ground black pepper.

Combine the cabbage, celery and onion together in a large bowl. Add the grated carrots and lemon juice and stir well. Mix the oil with the yoghurt, season to taste and pour over the salad ingredients, lifting and mixing gently until the vegetables are well coated. Cover and keep in a cool place for about an hour so that the flavours have time to 'marry'. If you prefer the texture to be slightly soft rather than very crisp, the coleslaw should be made a couple of hours ahead.

WALNUT AND AVOCADO SALAD
(Serves 4)

This makes an unusual starter, and as the mixture of nuts and avocado is high in protein, it is also good as a healthy light lunch along with another salad, such as lettuce, tomato, cucumber, celery, beansprouts and / or sliced orange – served with brown bread and butter.

    2 ripe avocado pears
    2 tbsp lemon juice
    2 dessert apples
    50 g / 2 oz walnuts or unsalted cashew nuts
    3 tbsp extra virgin olive oil
    2 cloves garlic
    Salt and freshly ground black pepper and (if serving as a starter) a few
    lettuce leaves and cucumber slices.

Cut the avocados in half, discard the stones and carefully scoop out the flesh, being careful not to damage the skin. Mash the avocado flesh with the lemon juice, stir in the oil, a little salt and pepper and the garlic (put through a garlic press or very finely chopped). Mix well, fold in the chopped walnuts or cashew nuts and the apples, peeled, cored and finely chopped, taste for seasoning. Pile the mixture back into the avocado shells, chill for up to 30 minutes and serve on individual plates garnished with lettuce and cucumber as a starter, or as a light lunch served with brown bread and butter.

SUMMERY STUFFED TOMATOES

(Allow 1 per person)

Rinse the required number of large tomatoes under the cold tap, cut off the top and scoop out the inside with a teaspoon, discard the seeds and then roughly chop the tomato centres to be mixed with your chosen filling.

Turn the 'cases' upside down to drain for about 20 minutes, season lightly inside with a little salt and freshly ground black pepper and fill with any of the following mixtures, top with the lids and serve on a bed of lettuce with plenty of brown bread and butter, for a light lunch or supper. Choose one of the following fillings to fill the tomato 'cases' then replace their lids:

- Finely chop 4 scallions (green tops too) and 1 stick celery and mash into 255 g / 8 oz cottage cheese along with the chopped tomato centres, ½ teaspoon made English mustard, and seasoning to taste – this is enough to fill 4 to 6 tomatoes.

- Try mixing in a tablespoon of chopped walnuts or unsalted cashew nuts for extra crunch or a spoonful of chopped red pepper (seeds discarded) for added colour and flavour.

- Mix cooked flaked fish – salmon, smoked haddock, cod, mackerel or tuna from a tin – with a raw onion and parsley, both finely chopped, and fold in plenty of mayonnaise (Miracle whip is good as it's low in calories and very popular with children), plus 2 or 3 tablespoons cooked rice and season to taste.

- Dice half a cucumber, 2 sticks celery, and half a red pepper (seeds discarded) and chop 3 shallots up into small pieces. Mix with 3 chopped hard-boiled eggs, season with salt and black pepper and fold in ½ cup plain yogurt and 2 tablespoons mayonnaise.

LENTIL AND WALNUT SALAD

(Serves 6)

2 cups dried red lentils – use a 250 ml cup for measuring

4 carrots

1 medium onion

3 cloves

4 cups chicken stock (or 1 chicken cube and water)

A small bay leaf

2 sprigs fresh thyme (or good pinch dried)

¼ cup each of white wine vinegar and olive oil

Salt, and freshly ground pepper

½ cup of finely sliced onions or leeks

½ cup chopped scallions (including green tops)

6 sticks celery

110 g / 4 oz walnut halves

Plenty of chopped parsley and some lettuce

Place the lentils, carrots cut into small cubes, onion studded with cloves, half a bay leaf and thyme in a saucepan with the chicken stock, and bring to the boil. Turn down the heat.

Lentil cooking times vary, so simmer gently, skimming off any froth, for about 15 minutes or longer until tender but still holding shape – if you over-cook they'll be mushy.

Meanwhile whisk the vinegar and oil together. When the lentils are done, drain through a sieve and discard the whole onion, cloves, bay leaf and thyme, and turn into a bowl.

Pour the oil and vinegar over while still hot, toss gently, season to taste, leave to get cold, then toss again before refrigeration overnight. About an hour before serving gently mix in the sliced onion or leeks, scallions and chopped celery and serve each portion on a bed of lettuce leaves, liberally sprinkled with chopped parsley for added colour and Vitamin C.

TUNA PASTA SALAD

(Serves 4)

This is much liked by teenagers – teach them to use a can opener and they might volunteer to make it for you.

350 g /12 oz green tagliatelle pasta

A small knob of butter,

200 g / 7 oz tin tuna

2 small onions finely sliced

2 tomatoes each cut into 6 wedges

2 hard-boiled eggs cut into quarters

I red pepper deseeded and diced

Small tin of sweetcorn (optional)

10 black or green olives (optional)

Cook the tagliatelle according to the instructions on the packet until 'al dente' (just soft to bite) but still firm. Drain well and dot with small flakes of butter which will melt and stop it sticking together. Leave to cool.

Make the dressing: mix 2 tablespoons wine vinegar, 2 tablespoons olive or Flora oil, salt and freshly ground black pepper together in an empty screw-top jar.

Add 2 tablespoons chopped scallions (green part too), 2 tablespoons chopped parsley and a clove of very finely chopped garlic (optional) and shake again.

Meanwhile flake the tuna lightly with a fork, being careful not to reduce it to a mush. Use two forks to toss the cooked pasta lightly with the tuna, onion, toma-toes, eggs, red pepper and / or peas and sweetcorn and olives if using. Pour the dressing over the pasta mixture and toss gently.

MIXED SALAD

A salad spinner is very useful for drying out lettuce after rinsing, leaving it crisp and ready for dressing.

Using rinsed and dried salad greens as a base, choose from the following to make individual combinations of flavour and colour: tomatoes, hard boiled eggs (halved bantam's eggs are particularly appealing), white turnip, small green peas, young carrots either sliced or grated, celery, spring onions, cucumber, radishes, sliced oranges, pineapple pieces, slices of unpeeled red apples (sprinkled with lemon juice to stop browning), thinly sliced green or red peppers (discard the seeds), florets of cauliflower.

Cooked vegetables such as potatoes sliced or cubed, carrots, peas, asparagus, green beans, artichoke hearts and beet root (well dried or the red juice will discolour the rest of the salad) can all be used. Garnish with sliced stuffed olives, capers, chopped herbs.

Arrange the chosen ingredients in a salad bowl or on a large flat dish.

MIXED GREEN SALAD

Choose your own selection of fresh green salad ingredients from the following: plenty of lettuce (butterhead, romaine, iceberg or others) torn into bite-sized pieces, rinsed and dried as above, chopped scallions, green pepper (seeds removed), courgette, celery cut into short thin strips, sliced avocado pear, a green apple cut into cubes with the skin still on; green grapes and a mixture of fresh chopped herbs such as parsley, marjoram, chives, tarragon and / or fennel.

Combine all together in a large salad bowl, add 6 to 8 slices of French bread brushed with extra virgin olive oil flavoured with crushed garlic (2 cloves to 3 tablespoons oil) – these are called chapons and really bring out the garlic flavour. Drizzle 2 or 3 tablespoons French dressing over and toss everything gently together, serve immediately. A generous sprinkling of toasted pinenuts is a delicious addition.

FRESH TOMATO SAUCE

This is quite different from ketchup and captures the taste of summer-ripened tomatoes perfectly.

These quantities yield about 600 ml / 1 pint sauce and it is lovely with grilled fish, chicken or meat and with beef burgers or sausages and chips.

Also very good added to soups casseroles and stews, so it worth making double or treble quantities while tomatoes are cheap, to be frozen in empty yoghurt or margarine containers, covered with polythene, or the lids.

    450 g / 1 lb ripe tomatoes
    1 small onion
    1 carrot
    ½ tsp sugar
    A good pinch of salt and a few grinds of black pepper, plus optional extras:
    1 clove of crushed garlic, 2 chopped rashers and / or a stick of celery,
    including leaves.

Cut up the tomatoes and chop or grate the onion and carrot. Place all the ingredients in a saucepan and simmer very gently for 30 minutes, with the lid on, stirring now and then.

Cool a little, whizz up in the blender or food processor for about 15 seconds, or until smooth then put through a sieve, to remove any bits of skin seeds etc. Taste for seasoning, reheat for immediate use, or package in small quantities for freezing, as above.

FRENCH DRESSING

    1 tbsp white wine vinegar
    3 tbsp olive oil – rapeseed or ground nut oil can be substituted
    Pinch of salt or more to taste
    1 clove garlic (optional)
    1 / 2 tsp French mustard and a tsp of castor sugar (optional)

Make double quantities if in constant demand as it keeps well in the refrigerator for a week or so.

Crush the garlic. Place with all other ingredients in a jar with a screw top lid, – and shake well. Shake before use as the vinegar separates from the oil on standing.

Variation:

(1) For a healthy dressing with a mixed and / or green leaf salad add 2 teaspoons finely chopped parsley mixed with chives, marjoram, dill, fennel, and / or raw onions plus a little sage or thyme, and leave for a couple of hours for the flavours to marry before using:

(2) For a well-flavoured new potato salad add a dessertspoon each of finely-chopped parsley, mint and raw onion, plus half a clove of very finely chopped garlic (if liked) to the oil and vinegar dressing, shake well and pour over hot sliced potatoes, leave to get cold before topping with mayonnaise.

WHITE SAUCE

25 g / 1 oz butter
25 g / 1 oz flour
300 ml (½ pint) milk
Salt and pepper

Melt the butter in a saucepan, mix in the flour until thickened, add milk by degrees stirring continuously and boil for about three minutes until smooth and creamy (the hand mixer is useful for removing any lumps).

A tiny pinch of mace or nutmeg, ½ teaspoon of mustard, chopped parsley or grated cheese may be added depending on the recipe, and a tablespoon of cream added at the last moment gives a velvety texture.

Parsley sauce – add 4 tablespoons of chopped parsley to the white sauce given above.

BEAUTIFUL PUDDINGS

Desserts and puddings round off a meal nicely. In earlier times they plugged the gaps and nourished the weak – as the recipe for Goody so amply shows. This is a lovely collection of my favourite recipes and I hope you enjoy going through them and trying them all out.

Puddings used to take a walk through the seasons – fruity in summer and autumn, spicy and bursting with dried fruit in winter, especially Christmas, and very plain indeed in spring. All that has changed as now we can buy almost anything we want out of season. Why not try eating puddings seasonally? You will find that often foods blend best together when they grow up together.

SUMMER PUDDING

225 g / 8 oz blackcurrants

4 tbsp water

225 g / 8 oz redcurrants

350 g / 12 oz raspberries

175 g / 6 oz castor sugar or to taste

A small wholemeal loaf

Strip the blackcurrants from their stalks with a fork; simmer gently with the water in a small covered saucepan for about 10 minutes. Keep about 10 small strings of redcurrants for garnish and strip the remainder, add these to the saucepan along with the raspberries and sugar. Simmer gently together, stirring now and then, until the sugar has melted and the berries are soft but not mushy. Leave to cool.

Butter a 900 ml / 1½ pint basin. Line the base and sides with wholemeal bread cut into medium-thick slices, crusts removed and slightly overlapping each other so that no gaps remain. Spoon the cooked berries into the bread-lined bowl, pour juice to within an inch of the top and keep the remainder.

Cover completely with more bread, trimmed to fit. Find a saucer which will fit inside the bowl on top of the bread. Place a weight – maybe a tin of beans or canned fruit – on the saucer and chill bowl and all in the refrigerator for at least 12 hours.

Just before serving run a knife between the bread lining and the basin to loosen the pudding, invert onto a serving dish with a raised edge which will not overflow with juice. Spoon the reserved juice over the pudding; decorate with strings of redcurrants on top and around the base.

RHUBARB CRUMBLE

Rhubarb is another of the tastes of long ago which have continued to be popular. When cooked it is a vibrant pink colour. It is one of the first fresh things to grow in spring, its wonderful tart flavour wakes up our winter-jaded taste buds with a bang!

You can use this crumble recipe with other fruit – cooking apples, gooseberries or plums. Use your freezer to store these fruits for crumbles when they're out of season.

900 g / 2 lb rhubarb

110 g / 4 oz sugar or more to taste

About 3 tbsp water

For the crumble topping:

75 g / 3 oz butter

175 g / 6 oz plain flour

75 – 110 g / 3–4 oz sugar

A good pinch ground cinnamon or ginger if liked.

Top and tail the rhubarb and chop into small chunks. Stew with the sugar and water in a covered saucepan, stirring occasionally until soft. Turn into a buttered 1.2 litre / 2 pint ovenproof dish. To make the crumble topping, rub the butter into the sifted flour until like breadcrumbs in consistency, add sugar and spice (if using) and run lightly through your fingers until well mixed.

Sprinkle the crumble evenly over the rhubarb, covering right to the edges of the dish, and press down very lightly. Place the dish in a baking tin containing about an inch of hot water – this is called a water-bath and stops the fruit boiling up through the topping. Bake for about 30 to 40 minutes in a very moderate oven 180C / 350F / Gas mark 4 until the crumble is golden brown on top.

Serve hot, with lots of hot runny Birds custard – Home-made is nicer and also cheaper than shop-bought in a ready-to-use carton!

BLACKBERRY FOOL

Very rich and luxurious, for special occasions only! Be sure to use a Quality Assured egg as this dessert is not cooked.

450 g / 1 lb blackberries, freshly picked or frozen

2 tbsp water mixed with 2 tsp cornflour or arrowroot

110 g / 4 oz castor sugar

300 ml / ½ pint double cream

1 egg white to increase the volume and lightness of the whipped cream.

Put the blackberries, cornflour (or arrowroot) mixture, sugar and water into a saucepan; cover with the lid and simmer gently for 10 minutes, or until soft.

Draw the pan off the heat and stir in the sugar which will dissolve in the hot juice. Press the contents of the saucepan, juice and all, though a nylon sieve into a mixing bowl and leave the puree to cool.

Whip the cream and egg white separately until thick and light and then combine. Fold the whipped mixture into the fruit puree quickly and lightly, using a metal tablespoon in a figure-of-eight movement.

Spoon the mixture into 6 serving glasses, chill for several hours or overnight, serve cold from refrigerator with boudoir sponge biscuits for dipping if liked.

NORA'S BAKED APPLES

Baked apples are extremely simple, very versatile, heart-warming on a cold day and surprisingly popular. An old friend tells me that, even in this day and age, her top favourite method is 'how we used to bake apples before we ever had ovens to do them in'.

'Some nights, about an hour before bedtime, I take a whole apple, without removing the core, and wrap it in a piece of butterpaper – the foil is best – and put it in the dying embers of the fire. It bakes away fine and I eat it hot with sugar and a little butter just before I go to bed – the real taste of the old days, lovely and full of flavour.'

4 evenly sized, fairly large apples

4 heaped dessertsp brown sugar

White or brown breadcrumbs made from 4 slices of bread

About 2 dessertsp sultanas

25 g / 1 oz butter

3 tbsp water

1 tbsp of sugar

Wash and dry the apples. Carefully remove the cores, and with the point of a sharp knife, slit the skin around the circumference just above the middle of each apple – this stops the skins bursting at random and the fluffy cooked apple showing in a ring around each apple looks most appetising.

Place side-by-side in a roasting dish or other ovenproof dish just large enough to fit, and spoon in the 3 tablespoons of water and 1 of sugar.

Fill the hollow centres with alternate layers of sugar, breadcrumbs, sultanas and small bits of butter, ending with butter.

Bake in a preheated oven 190C / 375F / Gas mark 5 for 40 to 45 minutes until the apples are soft right through. Serve hot, spooning the syrupy juice over the apples. For an unusual finish, place a marshmallow on top of each apple about 5 minutes before the end of cooking time, and leave it to melt and brown a little before serving.

Alternative fillings: use any of the following, and place a small knob of butter on top of the filling before baking – a mixture of chopped dates, sultanas, chopped dried apricots and / or mixed peel; chopped glace fruits, including cherries mixed with chopped walnuts for special occasions; mincemeat; or dried mango slices with crystallised ginger.

CHRISTMAS PUDDING MADE WITH CIDER

The essence of niche marketing is to have something different. Val and I were founder members of the Country Market in Fermoy, Co Cork and experimented with cider in our Christmas puddings instead of the usual ale or Guinness. They were so successful that we could hardly keep up with the demand!

Rich plum puddings like this can be made between 3 and 8 weeks ahead to allow time for them to mature. This mixture makes three 600 ml / pint-size puddings each enough for 6 servings, or 1 large and 1 small pudding.

450 g / 1 lb sultanas
350 g / 12 oz raisins
225 g / 8 oz currants
50 g / 2 oz blanched almonds chopped
110 g / 4 oz mixed peel
110 g / 4 oz glace cherries
225 g / 8 oz plain flour sifted with 1 level tsp each of mace, ginger and mixed spice (or failing this 3 tsp mixed spice)
Good pinch of salt
450 g / 1 lb soft light brown sugar
50 g / 2 oz ground almonds
225 g / 8 oz fresh bread crumbs (made in the blender if you have one)
110 g / 4 oz packaged shredded suet
6 eggs
Approximately 425 ml / ¾ pint cider

Grease the pudding bowls and put a disc of greaseproof paper at the base of each for easy turning-out – I always place 4 halved glace cherries cut-side down on the disk to give a rich look when it's turned out.

Place the sultanas, raisins, currants, chopped almonds and mixed peel in a bowl and run through your fingers; add the remaining cherries cut in half and sprinkled lightly with flour.

Sift the remaining flour, salt and spices into a large mixing bowl. Add the sugar, ground almonds, breadcrumbs, suet, mixed fruit, and run these dry ingredients through your fingers until well mixed. Beat the eggs, add 425 ml / ¾ pint of cider and whisk together. Pour into a well in the centre of the dry mixture and stir thoroughly, adding a little extra cider if the mixture is too stiff.

Now comes the magic moment for each member of the family to take a turn at stirring and to make a secret wish – according to superstition this brings luck to the house. Once this has been done you can divide the mixture evenly between the prepared bowls, leaving at least an inch of space up to the rim, and cover with the snap-on lid, or failing this a circle of greaseproof paper covered with a circle of foil tied securely in under the rim.

As the boiling time is so long it is often more convenient to do this the following morning. Place the bowls in individual saucepans, with boiling water coming halfway up the sides. Cover with foil tied around the saucepan to keep in the steam with the lid perched on top – this means you don't have to top-up with boiling water nearly so often.

Boil steadily, allowing 6 hours for the small puddings, 7 for the larger ones and topping up the water as necessary. When boiling time is completed take the puddings out of the saucepan, remove the snap-on lid or covering foil, and leave in a warm room for two days for the surface to dry out. Then cover again, and store in a cool dry place to mature and mellow in flavour until needed.

Before serving boil the pudding for another hour, turn out onto a serving plate, top with a sprig of holly. Flame the pudding by heating a tablespoon of brandy or whiskey over a candle, lighting with a match and pouring over the top of the pudding. Serve with brandy butter (see below) and whipped cream. In my experience lots of people, especially children, relish this very rich fruity pudding with hot, runny Bird's custard.

BRANDY BUTTER

110 g / 4 oz butter

225 g / 8 oz sifted icing sugar

2 tbsp brandy

Cream the butter until soft. Beat in the icing sugar a little at a time with the brandy until light and fluffy.

BAKED RICE PUDDING

(Serves 4)

Most people have forgotten what old-fashioned rice pudding actually tastes like, but it is beautifully creamy in texture due to the long slow cooking, which also brings out the lovely milky flavour.

600 ml milk / 1 pint

40 g / 1 ½ oz short-grain pudding rice

10 g / ½ oz butter

2 level tbsp castor sugar

A few drops vanilla essence

2 tbsp cream for special occasions

Heat the milk in a saucepan until just at boiling point. Meanwhile, place the rice in the base of a well-buttered 900 ml /1½ pint ovenproof dish, sprinkle in the sugar and add the butter, cut into small slivers. Pour in the hot milk, add the vanilla essence, and stir well together.

Bake on the shelf below the centre of a preheated very low oven 150C / 300F / Gas mark 2, and during the first 45 minutes make sure to stir the mixture three times at 15 minute intervals, to break up the skin forming on top. Stir in the cream (if using) at the third mixing, then bake for about an hour and 15 minutes longer (approximately 2 hours in all) without any further stirring, until rich and creamy with a golden skin on top.

MAISIE MILLAR'S PLUM PUDDING

This is a lovely old-fashioned steamed pudding that has been handed down in
Maisie Millar's family for generations.

900 ml / 1½ pint milk

10 g / ½ oz sago

110 g / 4 oz castor sugar

110 g / 4 oz margarine

225 g / 8 oz breadcrumbs (made in the blender if you have one)

1 large egg

1 level tsp bread soda

1 level tsp mixed spice

2 tsp lemon juice ('real lemon' from a bottle is handy)

225 g / 8 oz sultanas

25 g / 1 oz mixed peel

Place the sago in a sieve and rinse under the tap. Simmering it in the milk until the
grains are clear, add the margarine and stir until melted. Mix the breadcrumbs,
sifted bread soda, spice, sultanas and mixed peel together, stir in the sago mixture, beaten egg and lemon juice and mix well. Turn into a 15 – 18 cm / 6 – 7
inch greased pudding bowl, cover with greaseproof paper or the snap-on lid and
steam in a saucepan with water coming halfway up the sides for about 2 hours.
Turn out on to a round dish; serve with custard.

HOW TO MAKE GOOD MERINGUES

Meringues are everyone's favourite and simple to make, and they stay crisp in airtight tins for a week or longer so can be made ahead.

It's important to use eggs which are 2 or 3 days old – new laid don't whip up as well – the castor sugar must be bone dry and as the meringue mixture absorbs moisture it's a good idea to make them on a fine day. For best results use a deep Pyrex bowl for whisking in preference to a polythene one; rinse it and the electric beaters in hot water, dry well and leave to get cold before using.

Remove the eggs from the refrigerator the previous day, have ready a small bowl for the yolks as well as the deep one for the whites, and separate very carefully as even the tiniest trace of egg yolk prevents the whites from whipping properly. Always put the meringues onto the lowest runner in a preheated very low oven (about 100C / 200F / Gas mark ¼) immediately after they've been put onto the baking sheet – the aim is to dry them out rather than cook them.

The meringue mixture may be piped into equally sized shells – it is enough to make 10 to 12 shells 2 inches in diameter, fewer if they are larger – which are put together in pairs with whipped cream. Alternatively if you don't have a piping bag it is just as satisfactory to scoop out oval shapes onto the baking sheet using a tablespoon, dessertspoon or even a teaspoon according to the size you want.

Incidentally if the oven is slightly too hot, or the meringues have been left in too long they may be a pale golden colour and they're none the worse for that!

And waste not, want not – I use the egg yolks beaten up with 2 or 3 whole eggs, half teasp salt and freshly ground black pepper, poured into a heated pan with a knob of butter and made into a rich scrambled egg filling for sandwiches!

BASIC MERINGUE MIXTURE

3 egg whites
A tiny pinch (scant ⅛ of a teasp) of Bextartar
175 g / 6 oz castor sugar

First prepare the 2 baking sheets – line them with Raytex greaseproof paper cut to fit and held down at the corners with a smear of butter.

Whip the egg whites until frothy with an electric mixer, add the Bextartar and whip again until stiff, then add half the castor sugar a tablespoon at a time whipping between each addition – the texture will be fine and smooth with lots of tiny air bubbles, and will hold peaks.

Sprinkle the remaining sugar evenly into the bowl and continue to whisk until the mixture is stiff and shiny.

Place the meringue shells or ovals on to the baking sheet and put into the preheated very low oven as described previously, close the door gently and leave to dry out for 1½ to 2½ hours or longer according to size until very crisp and light.

Then loosen them carefully with a palette knife, turn onto their sides and leave in the turned off oven for another 30 minutes or so.

Join the ovals together in pairs with whipped cream or fill the shells with whipped cream and fresh fruit such as raspberries or strawberries. Store as described earlier if not for immediate use.

GOODY (TRADITIONAL)

This version of bread and milk for young and old was a great standby in many families in Ireland right up to the 1950s and very delicious it is too, as I learned years ago from a farmer's wife then in her late seventies. 'There were no baby foods way back in the old days, and when they came off the bottle the babies needed something soft and nourishing to eat. What we gave them was mashed potato and goody'.

'What you'd do was put a cupful or two of fresh bread crumbs into a small bowl, sprinkle a teaspoon of sugar on it (or more to taste) and pour enough boiling milk over to make it nice and thickish – it's for eating not drinking'.

'It was also very good for the old folk and truth to tell almost everyone in the family would love it. It was what we call "comfort food" nowadays I suppose,' she said.

I have a fellow feeling when it comes to Goody being comfort food because in far away South Africa up to the age of about 12 my mother gave me a bowl of warm bread and milk if I felt off colour or was upset about anything.

And come to think about it, maybe that's why old fashioned Bread and Butter Pudding and Queen of Puddings, both based on bread and milk, have come back into popularity over recent years.

BREAD AND BUTTER PUDDING
(Serves 4)

6 slices white bread
50 g / 2 oz butter,
50 g / 2 oz sultanas
50 g / 2 oz castor sugar
2 large eggs
600 ml / I pint milk
A little freshly grated nutmeg or a pinch of powdered mace

Remove and discard the crusts, and spread the bread with the butter before cutting each slice into four. Butter a square or rectangular 1.2 litre / 2 pint ovenproof dish and lay half the bread butter-side down in an even layer on the base. Sprinkle in all the sultanas and half the sugar.

Cover with the remaining bread, arranged butter-side-up in an even layer. Beat the eggs and milk together and strain through a sieve over the pudding.

Sprinkle the remaining sugar on top and dust very lightly with nutmeg or mace, then leave to stand for about half an hour. Bake in a preheated low oven 170C / 325F / Gas mark 3 for about 50 to 60 minutes until golden on top. Good served with hot runny custard or stewed apple.

Variation: sprinkle in 25 g / I oz grated dark chocolate with the other ingredients.

QUEEN OF PUDDINGS
(Serves 4)

Very simple, light and delicate in flavour, another family favourite based on bread and milk and good enough to serve when you're having friends in for a meal!

110 g / 4 oz white breadcrumbs

600 ml / 1 pint milk

50 g / 2 oz butter (nicer than margarine)

3 eggs yolks

½ tsp vanilla essence

75 g / 3 oz castor sugar

4 rounded tbsp apricot or raspberry jam

For the meringue topping:

3 egg whites

50 g / 2 oz castor sugar

Place the breadcrumbs in a lightly buttered shallow baking dish. Heat the milk and butter until just warm, add the beaten egg yolks, vanilla essence, and 75 g / 3 oz castor sugar and whisk lightly together.

Pour this mixture over the breadcrumbs and leave to stand for at least 30 minutes, or up to 4 hours if preparing ahead.

Bake in the centre of a preheated oven, 180C / 350F / Gas mark 4 for about 20 minutes or until the bread-custard has set. Remove from the oven and spread the jam over the pudding. Whisk the egg whites until stiff, fold in the 50 g / 2 oz castor sugar.

Pile the meringue on top of the pudding, swirling it into peaks with the handle of a teaspoon and return the pudding to the oven for another 10 to 15 minutes until golden and crisp on top.

GOLDEN APPLE BETTY

(Serves 4 – 6)

About 10 slices white bread
75 g / 3 oz butter
900 g / 2 lb cooking apples
75 g / 3 oz brown sugar or more to taste
1 tsp cinnamon if liked

Butter the bread slices (crusts removed if preferred) and cut into quarters. Grease a shallow oblong ovenproof dish and line the base with bread placed butter-side down. Peel, core and slice the apples, arrange half in an even layer over the bread, sprinkle with about a third of the sugar and a dusting of cinnamon if using.

Cover with another layer of bread, arrange the remaining apple in an even layer sprinkled with sugar and cinnamon and top with the remaining bread, butter-side up with edges slightly over-lapping to prevent the apple cooking through.

Sprinkle with the remaining sugar and cinnamon, cover the dish with foil and bake in a preheated very moderate oven 180C / 350F / Gas mark 4 for about 40 minutes. Remove the covering and put back into the oven for another few minutes until golden and crisp at the edges. Serve hot with lashings of hot runny custard.

BANANA CUSTARD

(Serves 4)

This was my brother Peter's favourite pudding.

600 ml / 1 pint milk

3 rounded tbsp sugar

3 bananas

½ tsp cinnamon (optional)

2 rounded tbsp custard powder

Mix the custard powder with a little of the milk until it is a thin smooth paste. Add the cinnamon and the sugar to the rest of the milk in a saucepan, bring to the boil and as it foams up pour all together into a bowl with the custard. Stir until it thickens. Slice the bananas and mix into the hot custard, serve hot or cold.

BAKED BANANAS

(Serves 4 – 6)

75 g / 3 oz brown sugar

6 bananas

300 ml / ½ pint orange juice

25 g / 1 oz butter

½ tsp mixed spice

2 tbsp sultanas

Grated rind of ½ an orange

3 tbsp rum (optional)

Peel the bananas, cut in half lengthwise and place in a flat oven proof dish, previously buttered. Heat the orange juice, brown sugar, sultanas, grated rind of the orange, and butter all together until syrupy, pour over the bananas. Bake for about 15 minutes in a hot oven (220C / 425F / Gas mark 7). Serve hot. If you are using the rum, heat it, set alight and pour over the pudding at the table. Delicious with vanilla ice cream.

PAVLOVA WITH FRUIT AND CREAM
(Serves 4 – 6)

This step by step recipe for Pavlova will come as a pleasant surprise to those who haven't previously made one, as it is so simple and quick to prepare, always brings compliments for the cook and costs comparatively little compared to other luxury desserts, a treat for the family and equally good if you're having friends in.

Crisp and pale golden outside, soft as a marshmallow within, and topped with fruit and whipped cream, this dessert looks as good as it tastes.

3 egg whites
Pinch salt
175 g / 6 oz castor sugar
½ tsp vanilla essence
1 tsp vinegar
1 tsp corn flour

For the topping:
1½ to 2 small cartons (170 ml size) cream
4 tsp icing sugar
A few drops vanilla essence
Plus fruit of your choice – fresh raspberries and / or strawberries, or tinned peaches and pineapple cut into small chunks garnished with halved de-seeded green grapes or sliced kiwi are good.

Remove the eggs from the refrigerator beforehand as they whip better at room temperature. Draw around a plate or cake tin to make a circular outline 20 cm / 8 inches in diameter on a square of non-stick baking parchment (Raytex) and lay this on a metal baking sheet – a tiny dab of butter under each corner helps to keep it lying flat.

Preheat the oven to 170C / 325F / Gas mark 3.

To make the meringue mixture: separate the eggs, reserving the yolks for another purpose. Beat the egg whites with a pinch of salt in a deep Pyrex (gives better results than polythene) bowl until stiff.

Sprinkle in the castor sugar a tablespoon at a time, whisking well between each addition and add the corn flour, vanilla essence and vinegar along with the final spoonful.

The secret of success is thorough beating each time so that the meringue is glossy, much increased in volume and really stiff. Spoon the mixture into the middle of the circle marked out on the parchment and use a palette knife to spread it into a flat even layer right up to the outline on the paper.

This is my special way, much nicer than the usual 'nest' shape with raised edges as you're not left with an uncovered circle around the sides and a too-thin layer of meringue underneath the cream topping.

Place immediately on the centre shelf of the preheated oven and bake for 45 minutes, then turn off the heat and leave in the oven with the door closed for at least 2 hours until completely cold. Peel off the parchment carefully and place on a serving plate.

Just before serving, whip the cream with the icing sugar and vanilla essence until it holds peaks and spread evenly over the Pavlova base, and arrange the chosen fruit on top – luscious and appetising!

WINDY PUDDING
(Serves 4)

So easy to make; and very popular with the young who find the name hilarious.

  1 pkt strawberry jelly
  300 ml / ½ pint evaporated milk, chill in the fridge for about 2 hours
  before use
  425 ml / ¾ pint hot water

Dissolve the jelly in the boiling water, leave till cold but not set. Whip the evaporated milk until stiff, fold gently into the jelly, making sure it is well blended. Leave in a cool place to set.

HOT PINEAPPLE PUDDING
(Serves 4 – 6)

A family favourite recipe which goes down a treat with everyone we know. N.B. If you're using tinned pineapple unsweetened in its own juice more sugar should be added to taste.

  225 g / 8 oz tin of pineapple chunks, or failing this pineapple slices cut into chunks
  25 g / 1 oz butter
  25 g / 1 oz plain flour
  25 g / 1 oz castor sugar (double this if you have a sweet tooth)
  2 egg yolks
  1 tbsp lemon juice

For the meringue topping:

  2 egg whites
  75 g / 3 oz castor sugar
  Reserved pineapple pieces and a little green angelica for decoration

Drain the juice from the tin into a measuring jug, add the lemon juice and enough water to make up to 300 ml / ½ pint. Melt the butter in a saucepan, stir in the flour and cook over low heat for 1 minute stirring all the time.

Gradually beat in the juice from the tin, bring to the boil and cook for about 5 minutes still stirring continuously until you have a smooth sauce.

Remove from heat and allow to cool a little before beating in the egg yolks and sugar.

Stir in the drained pineapple chunks, reserving about 6 for decoration, turn the mixture into a well-buttered Pyrex dish. Beat the egg whites until stiff, whisk in the sugar, then spoon the meringue mixture evenly over the pudding, flicking it into peaks with the blade of a knife.

Decorate with reserved pineapple chunks and small pieces of angelica and bake in a low oven 180C / 350F / Gas mark 3 for about 15 minutes until pale golden on top. Gorgeous served hot with whipped cream!

MRS SALTER'S COFFEE MOUSSE
(Serves 4)

This recipe for Coffee Mousse was originally given to me by Mrs Vera Salter. It is so light it could fly straight to heaven! The mousse has a lovely smooth texture although, surprisingly enough, it contains neither eggs nor cream. It is also very simple to make and comes in handy for emergency entertaining as the ingredients can be kept in the stock cupboard and it sets in about 20 minutes!

1 tin evaporated milk (Ideal or Carnation 410 g size)

½ a teacup water

1 envelope gelatine (1 pint sachet)

3 tsp Irel coffee essence

½ tsp vanilla essence

Approximately 50 g / 2 oz castor sugar or to taste, see below.

If time allows, chill the tin of evaporated milk in the refrigerator for a couple of hours before using. Pour the evaporated milk into a 1.8 litre / 3 pint Pyrex bowl then whip until thick and creamy and very much increased in volume. Shake the powdered gelatine into the ½ cup of water, place this in a saucepan of hot water and stir briskly until completely dissolved.

Pour the dissolved gelatine in a thin stream into the whipped evaporated milk, beating continuously – I use an electric hand-mixer and go on beating until the mixture has increased in volume to about 1.2 litre / 2 pints, very light and full of air.

Add the coffee essence, vanilla and castor sugar; beat again until thoroughly mixed then taste to see if a little more castor sugar or Irel is needed to suit your own preference.

Turn into a pretty glass dish, chill in the refrigerator until needed, decorate with walnut halves and/or swirls of cream if liked.

GOLDEN SYRUP PUDDING
(Serves 4)

In our house this is always very popular with the men and boys of the family.

  110 g / 4 oz margarine
  110 g / 4 oz castor sugar
  2 large eggs
  110 g / 4 oz self-raising flour, sifted
  4 tbsp golden syrup
  An extra 4 tbsp syrup and 1 tbsp water for the sauce

Cream the margarine and castor sugar and add the eggs one at a time, sprinkling in a little flour with each one; then gently folding in the remainder of the flour.

Grease a 900 ml / 1 ½ pint pudding basin, put the syrup on the bottom, and then spoon in the sponge mixture. Level the surface, cover with the snap-on lid or use buttered foil pleated across the centre to allow for rising and well tied in around the rim.

Steam for one and three quarter hours in a saucepan with simmering water coming half-way up the sides of the bowl, covered with the lid to keep the steam in.

Make sure the pan does not boil dry. When done, heat the syrup and water in a small pan, turn the pudding out onto a dish with a raised edge and pour the hot sauce over. Serve with lashings of hot runny Birds custard.

FESTIVE APPLE PUDDING
(Serves 4 – 6)

This recipe alternates between layers of fruit and sponge. It is a very good alternative for people who don't like Christmas pudding – actually it goes down well at any time of year.

Eating apples are better than cookers for this recipe because they give a delectable 'whole fruit' texture as they don't break down to a pulp during cooking.

225 g / 8 oz dessert apples (weighed after peeling and coring),

110 g / 4 oz sultanas

25 g / 1 oz mixed peel

50 g / 2 oz glace cherries

2 level tbsp Demerara sugar

1 level tsp ground cinnamon

110 g / 4 oz butter or margarine

110 g / 4 oz castor sugar

2 eggs

175 g / 6 oz self-raising flour sifted with 1 level tsp baking powder

2 tbsp milk

Cut the apples into ½ inch dice after peeling and coring and put into a bowl with the sultanas, peel, halved cherries, Demerara sugar and cinnamon. Mix well.

In another bowl cream the butter or margarine and sugar, beat in the eggs one at a time adding a light sprinkling of flour with the second one, then fold in the remaining flour and milk by degrees.

Spoon half the fruit mixture into a lightly buttered 1.2 litre / 2 pint pudding bowl lined on the base with a circle of greaseproof paper. Top with about half the creamed mixture and smooth the surface level before adding the second layer of fruit mixture, followed by the remaining creamed mixture.

The bowl shouldn't be more than about two thirds full. Cover in the usual way with a snap-on lid or 2 layers of greaseproof paper tied in tightly around the rim, then steam for 2 hours, standing on an upturned saucer or scone cutter, in a saucepan with gently boiling water coming about half way up the sides of the bowl. Make sure the pan does not boil dry! Turn out onto a large plate, discard the paper disc, and serve hot with plenty of hot runny custard or whipped cream for special occasions

LIGHT LEMON MOUSSE
(Serves 4)

This is another of my favourite desserts, light and airy, so smooth in consistency that guests invariably think it is loaded with cream – fortunately it isn't as fattening as that. It's very important to use eggs stamped with the Irish Quality Assurance mark as this dessert is not cooked.

   3 egg yolks

   4 egg whites

   I dessertsp powdered gelatine

   I tbsp cold water

   175 g / 6 oz castor sugar

   5 tbsp lemon juice

   2 tbsp hot water

Put the gelatine into a cup with the tablespoon of cold water. Whisk the egg yolks, castor sugar and lemon juice together for at least 10 minutes until the mixture holds a trail when the beaters are drawn across the surface – I use an electric hand mixer. Add the 2 tablespoons hot water to the gelatine and stand the cup in a small pan of water over a low heat until the gelatine is completely dissolved. Continue to whisk the egg / lemon mixture while pouring the melted gelatine onto the rotating beaters; go on beating for a couple of minutes longer until thoroughly mixed in.

Using another bowl and clean beaters, whisk the 4 egg whites until stiff. Fold gently into the mixture with a metal tablespoon until so well mixed that no white streaks remain. Turn into a pretty glass dish, chill until needed. Decorate with halved cherries and small strips of angelica if liked before serving.

Tip: it is easier to squeeze all the juice from a lemon if it is slightly softened by rolling on a hard surface, or alternatively warmed for 2 minutes in a moderate oven before you cut it in half.

STRAWBERRY CITRUS SORBET

450 g / 1 lb strawberries

Juice of 1 lemon and 1 orange

300 ml / ½ pint water

225 g / 8 oz castor sugar

2 egg whites (use Quality Assured eggs as this dessert is not cooked)

Liquidise the strawberries in batches in the blender with the lemon and orange juice, then pass the puree through a nylon sieve to remove the tiny pips.

Stir the sugar and water in a saucepan over a low heat until the sugar has completely dissolved, bring up to the boil and then remove from the heat. Stir in the strawberry puree, leave to cool completely before pouring into a freezer container.

Freeze without covering until a layer of ice forms around the edges of the container. Whisk the egg whites until stiff. Turn the half-frozen slushy strawberry mixture into a chilled mixing bowl, add the beaten egg whites and whisk until smooth, light and thick.

Turn the mixture into the freezer container and freeze for 4 hours or so until firm, cover with the lid and return to the freezer until needed. Spoon straight from the freezer into pretty glasses as individual servings, a leaf of lemon balm or sprig of mint make a nice garnish.

BLACKCURRANT SORBET

Sorbets were served between courses at grand dinner parties to refresh the guests' palates; nowadays they are often eaten as an alternative to ice cream.

225 g / 8 oz fresh or frozen blackcurrants

110 g / 4 oz castor sugar

300 ml / ½ pint water plus more as needed

2 level tsp powdered gelatine soaked in 2 tbsp water

1 tsp lemon juice

2 egg whites (use Quality Assured eggs as this dessert is not cooked)

Heat the water and sugar over a low heat, stirring until the sugar has dissolved, then boil gently for 10 minutes. Draw off the heat, stir in the soaked gelatine until dissolved and leave to cool – the gelatine gives a smooth texture and stops the mixture freezing too hard and solid.

Meanwhile gently simmer the fresh or frozen blackcurrants (stripped from their stalks) in 2 tablespoons water, with the lid on, for about 10 minutes or so until tender.

Rub the currants through a nylon sieve before mixing with the syrup or, easier still, mix with the cooled syrup and whizz up in the blender before sieving to remove tiny pips.

Add extra water to make up to 600 ml / 1 pint and leave to cool. Stir in the lemon juice, and freeze in ice cube trays minus the dividers in the refrigerator freezing compartment, or in a shallow container in the freezer, until icy but still rather mushy.

Whisk the egg whites until stiff but not dry, turn the fruity mixture into a chilled bowl and whisk briskly until well broken up. Fold in the egg whites, and freeze again until firm – cover if the sorbet is to be stored in the freezer for use later on. Spoon straight from the freezer into small chilled serving dishes or glasses.

FAMILY FAVOURITE ICE CREAM

(8 large servings or 10 – 12 smaller ones)

Most home-made ice creams require beating at frequent intervals during the freezing process to prevent crystals forming, but this particular ice cream, brought into the family by daughter Rosalie's husband Kevin, needs no attention after the initial mixing. It's easy to make, smooth and creamy, much more delicious than commercial ice cream and the best I've ever tasted. As it contains raw egg use Quality Assured eggs.

300 ml / ½ pint whipping cream
4 large eggs (Quality Assured)
Small pinch of salt
110 g / 4 oz icing sugar
½ tsp vanilla essence
2 or 3 tbsp of grated chocolate can be added if liked

Carefully separate the eggs, placing the whites in a large bowl and the yolks in a small one. Add a small pinch of salt to the egg whites and beat until stiff – I use an electric hand mixer. Add the sifted icing sugar a dessertspoonful at a time, and beat well between additions so as to incorporate as much air as possible. When it has all been added beat the egg yolks with the vanilla essence and fold gently into the meringue mixture using a metal tablespoon in a figure-of-eight movement.

Whip the cream until it holds soft peaks, being careful not to over-beat as it shouldn't be too stiff, and turn into the bowl. Use a metal tablespoon to fold the whipped cream into the meringue mixture, working very gently and quickly so that the consistency stays light and full of air.

To Freeze: Immediately after mixing turn the ice cream into 1 or 2 large poly-thene containers with snap-on lids – empty margarine or ice cream containers are ideal. Freeze at lowest temperature for 6 to 8 hours, then store in the freezer until needed.

Spoon out individual servings as required, lovely on its own on a hot day or with hot apple tart, dark rich chocolate cake, fruit salad, lemon mousse or other sum-mery desserts. Also very good with Carolan's Irish Cream Liqueur spooned over the top for special occasions.

BEST EVER FRUIT SALAD

All too often when dining out you find the 'Fresh Fruit Salad' proudly featured on the menu has too much chopped apple in it and is awash with sugar syrup.

My fruit salad is based on a tin of Lustre pineapple in pineapple juice (no sugar added), net weight 425 g, with any additional juice required coming from a packet of unsweetened pineapple juice – the only kind that works without discolouring.

No sugar is added, and nothing else goes into it apart from fresh fruit in season chosen according to preference, and cut up into walnut size pieces so that the flavour and texture of the various fruits can be savoured separately. I've chosen a yellow and green theme for the recipe given below but you can choose your own combinations according to taste.

YELLOW AND GREEN FRUIT SALAD
(Serves 6 – 8)

Put it together as follows: put the unsweetened juice and slices of pineapple from a 425 g Lustre brand tin, cut unto chunks in a large glass bowl.

Wash 2 or 3 large oranges and cut up as given below, add to the bowl; follow with half a large ripe pineapple – cut into slices, skin and cores discarded and flesh cut into pieces; peeled mandarins – divide into sections and add to the bowl; wash and thinly peel 2 ripe mangoes and cut into chunks; add about 225 g / ½ lb seedless green grapes, well washed and cut in half lengthways for eye appeal and extra flavour, plus 3 ripe kiwis, skins removed, cut into fairly thick slices – divide these into thirds for a darker shade of green if liked.

Pour in unsweetened pineapple juice from a carton if needed, and serve with vanilla ice cream, whipped cream or spoonfuls of Fuchsia brand crème fraiche which has a lovely texture and unusual flavour.

Other fruits that are good in a fruit salad: 3 or 4 ripe pears – peeled, cored and cut into chunks; 2 or 3 ripe bananas – peeled and sliced fairly thickly; ripe peaches, nectarines and / or plums – wash under the tap, cut into pieces and discard pips.

(NB: stripping the furry skin from ripe peaches starting at the stem end makes the texture more palatable when you eat them). Red grapes give lovely colour and a burst of taste when you bite into them.

Topical Tip: the easiest and most efficient way to cut up an orange, not only for inclusion in fruit salad, but to serve in small quantities for breakfast or as a dessert to children up to the age of 3 or 4 who tend to choke on the membrane covering the sections, is as follows: wash the unpeeled orange, cut in half lengthways with a sharp knife, then into quarters and then eighths.

Lay each section on a wooden board peel side down, and still using the sharp knife cut sharply downwards 4 times along the length to meet the white pith, then cut away the orange pieces by running the knife along the length of each skin. Once mastered, this is a useful trick for busy mums; I learnt it from my sister-in-law Elspeth Gardiner when our children were little.

STRAWBERRIES – my favourite luxury

There couldn't be anything more summery than fresh, ripe Irish-grown strawberries in June either popped into your mouth one by one, or with a sprinkling of sugar and whipped cream. In this case, especially if the berries are a little under-ripe, it's a good idea to cut off any white bits then cut into halves or quarters if large. Place in a pretty bowl and sprinkle fairly lightly with granulated rather than castor sugar for that little extra grittiness, and leave for an hour or two to draw the juice and sweeten the fruit.

Like bananas, strawberries and other berried fruits are high in potassium and are an excellent cheerer-upper if you're feeling down!

STRAWBERRY SAUCE

225 g / 8 oz fresh strawberries
75 g / 3 oz castor sugar
2 tbsp lemon juice

Whizz up all the ingredients together in the blender, serve chilled with cheesecake, lemon mousse or vanilla ice cream.

LEMON CHEESECAKE
(Serves 4 – 5)

This is the simplest cheesecake of all, everyone likes it because the lemon topping gives a refreshing tang.

    150 g / 5 oz Marie biscuits
    150 g / 5 oz castor sugar
    110 g / 4 oz melted butter
    225 g / 8 oz full-fat cream cheese (Philadelphia)
    3 tbsp lemon juice
    ½ a lemon jelly tablet
    About a cup of water
    1½ level tsp corn flour
    Large knob of butter

Place the biscuits in a polythene bag and crush into evenly sized crumbs with a rolling pin. Mix in a small bowl with 50 g / 2 oz of castor sugar and the melted butter and use to line the base and sides of an 8 inch loose-bottomed flan ring (or a flan ring set on a plate), pressing the crumb mixture firmly into place with the back of a dessert spoon.

Cut the half jelly tablet up into small pieces, place in a measuring jug and make up to a 150 ml / ¼ pint with boiling water, stir briskly until dissolved, leave to cool while you beat the cream cheese with 75 g / 3 oz of the castor sugar.

When the jelly is just beginning to set to the consistency of unbeaten egg white, add a little at a time to the cream cheese mixture, beating after each addition until all has been used. Pour into the flan case and chill in the refrigerator until set.

To make the lemon topping, put the 3 tablespoons lemon juice into a measuring jug, make up to 150 ml / ¼ pint with cold water. Use a little of this to blend the corn flour into a smooth paste, stir in the rest of the liquid along with the remaining sugar and bring to the boil in a small saucepan. Stir constantly for about 3 minutes until the mixture thickens and clears, remove from the heat and stir in the butter. Leave to cool to blood heat and spoon in an even layer over the cheese filling. Return completed cheesecake to the fridge and continue chilling until required, remove the flan ring (if using) before serving.

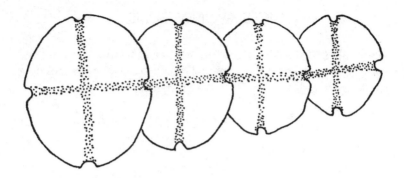

BOUNTIFUL BAKING

One of the pleasures of life; baking is very grounding and cheering for both cook and the rest of the family. The smell of bread baking or a sponge freshly out of the oven brings people together, anxious not to miss out on a real treat.

Rosalie, who is gluten intolerant, still continues to bake and as she can't taste anything she makes, she has to take critical feedback from the family acting in an advisory capacity. Three gluten-free recipes she regularly uses are included in this chapter.

Experience has taught me to listen to my cakes, especially the fruit ones, for when the buzzy sound that I call the 'singing' stops! If it has stopped it's time to test the cake with a skewer to make sure it's done – it should come out clean of crumbs when the cake is done.

For information: Bread soda in known as bicarbonate of soda, and Bextartar as cream of tartar.

ICED SPONGE BUNS

The first thing my children learnt to bake was sponge buns, usually eaten straight out of the oven as soon as they were cool enough to handle! This recipe doubles up successfully and can be used to make a plain sponge cake.

110 g / 4 oz margarine

110 g / 4 oz self-raising flour

110 g / 4 oz castor sugar

2 eggs

½ tsp vanilla essence

Glace cherries, enough for a half per bun

Preheat your oven to 200C / 400F / Gas mark 6. Set out bun tins and place a paper bun case in each space. Using a hand mixer cream the margarine and sugar until light and fluffy; beat in the vanilla and then the eggs one at a time, sprinkle in a teaspoonful of the flour before adding the second one.

Continue to beat with a metal tablespoon as using a mixer after the flour is added makes the buns tough. Put a dessertspoonful into each paper case, and bake for about 15 minutes, checking after 12 minutes as the buns may brown suddenly – again it's a good idea to make a note of the exact time needed in your oven.

Our offspring loved these buns straight from the oven, but if preparing ahead transfer to a wire grid and leave to cool. Put a halved glace cherry in the centre of each, or decorate with glace icing and then put the cherry on top!

GLACE ICING – any colour, any cake.

The icing sugar must be lump free, so crush 225 g / 8 oz icing sugar between two sheets of greaseproof paper with a rolling pin, sift into a bowl and mix in 1 ½ to 2 tablespoons of boiling water beating quick and hard – it should be liquid enough to spread with a knife blade.

Working rapidly as this icing sets very quickly, ice half the buns with white icing, add a scant drop of cochineal for pink icing or brown it with cocoa if preferred. These buns are nicest if eaten the same day although they can be kept in an airtight tin for a couple of days.

AN UNUSUAL RICH FRUIT CAKE

I was given this cake recipe by a keen cook in Australia. She was surprised I'd not come across it before, as in her family it was called Irish Christmas Cake! I like the method of soaking the fruit before making the cake but I changed the ingredients to suit my own taste. I hope you like it as much as I do.

50 g / 2 oz prunes

75 g / 3 oz dates

75 g / 3 oz glacé cherries

25 g / 1 oz glacé pineapple

50 g / 2 oz mixed peel

350 g / 12 oz raisins

350 g / 12 oz sultanas

1 tsp each grated rind from a well-scrubbed lemon and orange

2 tbsp lemon juice

5 tbsp orange juice

3 tbsp whiskey (use sherry or more orange juice if preferred)

2 heaped tbsp grated apple

25 g / 1 oz chopped walnuts

50 g / 2 oz ground almonds

175 g / 6 oz butter

175 g / 6 oz castor sugar

3 large eggs,

225 g / 8 oz plain flour, sifted with ½ tsp mace

(or 1½ tsp mixed spice)

A pinch of salt

1 extra tbsp whiskey

Stone and chop the prunes, chop the dates, quarter the cherries and cut the glacé pineapple to about the same size. Put in a large jar, or other container with a well-fitting lid. Add the peel, raisins, sultanas, lemon and orange rind and juice, whiskey and grated apple. Stir well until thoroughly mixed and leave to steep in the juices for anything from 3 days to a week, stirring every day. This gives a rich flavour and plumps up the dried fruit nicely.

Line a deep 20 cm / 8 inch square tin with two thicknesses of greaseproof paper (don't use foil instead) on base and sides, bringing it 5 cm / 2 inches above the rim, butter the paper on the inside. Pin two thicknesses of brown paper round the outside of the tin and place four thicknesses of brown paper or a flattened cereal carton on the baking sheet.

Beat the butter until soft, add the sugar and beat only until combined. Add the eggs one at a time, sprinkling in a little flour with each egg and beat well. Then fold in the chopped walnuts and ground almonds, followed by the sifted flour and spices. Finally stir in the prepared fruit, mixing well until thoroughly combined, spoon into the prepared tin, level the surface and top with split almonds if liked.

Bake on the centre shelf of a very low oven 150C / 300F / Gas mark 2 for 3 to 3½ hours, covering with greaseproof paper after 2 hours if getting too brown, and turning the heat down to 140C / 275F / Gas mark 1 for the final hour or so. Check that it's done with a warm skewer thrust into the centre, which should come out clean of crumbs.

Remove immediately from the oven. Prick the top lightly with a skewer and drizzle the extra tablespoon of whiskey over the top, cover with foil and leave to cool in the tin. Leave the lining paper in place, wrap in foil and store in an airtight tin for at least a week, or up to a month, before use.

WHITE CHRISTMAS CAKE

Make this cake only about two or three weeks ahead as it is not intended for long keeping.

110 g / 4 oz glace pineapple (failing that dried sweetened pineapple)

175 g / 6 oz glace cherries

110 g / 4 oz sultanas

50 g / 2 oz crystallised ginger

25 g / 1 oz mixed peel

25 g / 1 oz / angelica

50 g / 2 oz chopped walnuts

225 g / 8 oz plain flour

50 g / 2 oz corn flour

1 level tsp baking powder

Good pinch salt

225 g / 8 oz butter

150 g / 5 oz castor sugar

3 large eggs

1 tsp lemon juice

2 tsp brandy (optional)

2 – 3 tbsp milk

Rinse the pineapples, cherries, ginger and angelica in warm water to get rid of the sugary coating, dry gently on kitchen paper and cut into pieces about the size of half a cherry, except for the angelica, which is cut into thin strips.

Sift 2 tablespoons of the flour over the prepared fruit, mix in the chopped peel and walnuts, set aside until needed. Cream the butter with the sugar until light and fluffy, beat in the eggs one at a time, adding a sprinkling of the flour to prevent curdling.

Sift the flour with the corn flour, baking powder and salt, and fold lightly into the creamed mixture, alternating with the lemon juice, brandy and just enough milk to give a dropping consistency.

Fold in the prepared fruit and nuts, spoon the mixture into an 18 cm / 7 inch round cake tin, greased and lined inside with greaseproof paper. Bake in a low oven 170C / 325F / Gas mark 3, on the second rung from the bottom, for about 2½ hours until a skewer thrust into the centre comes out clean. Allow to cool in the tin for about 20 minutes and then turn onto a wire rack to cool, leave the lining paper in position and store in an airtight tin until needed.

SCANDINAVIAN APPLE CAKE

Quite different in taste and texture from the Irish equivalent, this goes down well with everyone!

   3 eggs
   250 g / 9 oz castor sugar
   110 g / 4 oz butter
   300 ml / ½ pint plus 1 tbsp full-cream milk,
   200 g / 7 oz plain flour sifted with a level tsp of baking powder
   4 good sized cooking apples

Whisk the eggs and 225 g / 8 oz of the castor sugar until thick and fluffy enough to hold a trail when the whisk is drawn across the surface.

Place the cut-up butter and milk in a small saucepan, bring up to the boil and while still bubbling pour into the whisked mixture, stirring briskly all the time.

Using a metal tablespoon, gently and carefully fold in the sifted flour until you have a smooth, lump-free batter. Pour the batter into a well-greased 20x30 cm / 8x12 inch roasting tin; scatter the peeled and cored sliced apples evenly across the surface and sprinkle the remaining sugar over.

Bake on the centre shelf of a preheated moderately hot oven at 400F / 200C / Gas mark 6 for about 25 minutes or so until well-risen and nicely browned. Cool in the tin before cutting into squares, serve with custard or whipped cream.

BOILED PINEAPPLE CAKE

Quite different in taste, texture and method, this cake is a nice addition to anyone's repertoire.

    400 g / 14 oz tin of crushed pineapple
    450 g / 1 lb mixed dried fruit
    110 g / 4 oz cherries
    50 g / 2 oz mixed peel
    110 g / 4 oz butter (gives you a better flavour and aroma
    than margarine)
    225 g / 8 oz sugar
    1 tsp bread soda
    3 eggs
    450 g / 1 lb plain flour
    1 tsp mixed spice
    1 tbsp whiskey or sherry

Put the crushed pineapple (including the juice) into a largish saucepan along with the dried fruit, halved cherries, peel, butter cut into small pieces, sugar and bread soda. Bring gently to the boil, stirring frequently to stop the mixture from catching on the bottom.

Once it starts to bubble turn down the heat and simmer for 3 minutes. Remove from the cooker and leave until the mixture is luke warm. Sift the flour with the spice and add to the saucepan a little at a time, alternating with the beaten eggs. Stir in the whiskey or sherry.

Turn into a square 20 cm / 8 inch tin, greased and lined with two layers of baking parchment on the bottom, and also around the sides projecting 5 cm / 2 inches above the rim of the tin.

Level the surface of the mixture, then make a shallow depression in the centre to allow for rising. Pin a double layer of brown paper around the side of the tin. Place on 4 sheets of brown paper or a layer of cardboard (a flattened cornflake box is fine) on the lowest shelf of a preheated oven 170C / 325F / Gas mark 3.

Bake for 1 hour and 20 minutes before turning the temperature down to 150C / 300F / Gas mark 2 for a further 30 minutes or so until done, covering with two layers of greaseproof paper if the top is getting too brown. Test in the usual way with a warm skewer thrust into the centre of the cake which should come out clean of crumbs.

Leave the cake in the tin to cool for 20 minutes before turning out onto a wire rack to cool. This is a moist well-flavoured cake which makes a pleasant change from the usual rich dark fruit cakes at Christmas, particularly for those who prefer to leave their baking until the last minute, as it needs only a few days to mature!

MY VERY SPECIAL CHOCOLATE CAKE

This was served at my daughter Rosalie's wedding and has been constantly requested by readers of my 'Countrylife' column in the *Irish Examiner*. Several times over the years to my certain knowledge the recipe has been used for a three tier wedding cake. This cake is not designed for keeping.

225 g / 8 oz plain flour
1 level tsp bread soda
½ tsp salt
50 g / 2 oz Bourneville cocoa
110 g / 4 oz butter
225 g / 8 oz castor sugar
2 large eggs
1 tbsp white vinegar
300 ml / ½ pint milk
1 tsp vanilla essence

For the very rich icing:

40 g / 1½ oz butter
1 egg yolk (Quality Assured)
450 g / 1 lb icing sugar
50 g / 2 oz Bourneville cocoa
4 tbsp cream
½ tsp vanilla essence

Sift the dry ingredients – flour, bread soda, salt and castor sugar – into a large bowl. Mix the vinegar with the milk and vanilla essence, put the eggs into this mixture, then pour into the dry ingredients and beat well. Add the butter (previously melted over low heat, then cooled) and beat again – the consistency should be like thick batter. Pour into a round cake tin 25 cm / 10 inches in diameter and lined round sides and base with greaseproof paper.

Bake in a very moderate oven 180C / 350F / Gas mark 4 for about 60 minutes or longer, covering with a double sheet of greaseproof paper if over-browning after 40 minutes. Test with a warm skewer thrust into the centre. Leave in the tin to cool for about 15 minutes before turning onto a wire rack to cool.

For the icing: cream the egg yolk and butter, add the vanilla essence, then the sieved icing sugar and cocoa, a little at a time, alternating with the cream, beating between each addition until the icing is light and fluffy – I use a hand-held electric mixer, as the texture is spoilt if over-beaten in a food processor. Insert four toothpicks halfway up the sides of the cake to act as guides, and slice into two even layers.

Sandwich together with a thick layer of chocolate icing, spread the remainder over the top and sides, reserving a little for piped decorations with an icing syringe. Arrange halved cherries and walnuts around the edge or, if this cake is to be used instead of the traditional rich fruit cake at Christmas time, set a red candle in a holder in the centre.

MY FAMILY'S FAVOURITE FRUIT CAKE

As well as being used at Easter and Christmas, this cake has been baked for family christenings and other celebrations over the years. As none of the family really likes Royal icing and marzipan, I decorate it with a colourful frill around the sides.

225 g / 8 oz butter

225 g / 8 oz brown sugar

4 large eggs

275 g / 10 oz sultanas

225 g / 8 oz raisins

175 g / 6 oz currants

110 g / 4 oz glace cherries

110 g / 4 oz mixed peel

50 g / 2 oz roughly chopped walnuts (American walnuts are the best if you can find them)

225 g / 8 oz plain flour sifted with 1 tsp each ground mace and cinnamon

2 tbsp brandy, whiskey or sherry, or water at a pinch

For best results all the ingredients should be at room temperature so take the butter and eggs out of the refrigerator well beforehand. Before you start mixing, butter the cake tin – you can use either a 18 cm / 7 inch square tin or a 20 cm / 8 inch round one – and line the base and sides with two layers of baking parchment which should project 2 inches above the top rim, then pin a double thickness of brown paper around the outside of the tin.

Wash the cherries to remove the syrup, dry well, cut in half and dust lightly with flour – this helps to prevent them sinking during baking. Turn on the oven to 150C / 300F / Gas mark 2 just before you start mixing.

Place the cut up butter and sugar in the mixing bowl, previously warmed under the hot tap and dried well, and cream them with an electric hand mixer. Beat the eggs together in another bowl and add to the creamed mixture a tablespoon at a time, beating well between additions and adding a dessertsp of sifted flour each time to prevent curdling.

When all the beaten egg has been added, use a metal tablespoon to fold in the remaining flour (previously sifted with the spices) a tablespoon at a time alternating with handfuls of the dried fruit mixed with halved cherries, peel and chopped nuts.

Finally add the brandy, whiskey, sherry or water and mix thoroughly to distribute the fruit evenly, but do not beat at this stage – if too stiff add a little extra liquid. Spoon the mixture into the prepared tin, pressing it well into the corners and using a rubber scraper to get all the mixture from the bowl, then make a shallow saucer shaped depression in the centre with the back of the tablespoon to allow for rising.

Place the cake tin on a metal baking sheet lined with 4 thicknesses of newspaper or a flattened cereal box, on the rung below the centre of a preheated cool oven 150C / 300F / Gas mark 2. Bake for about 3¾ hours – in my experience fruit cakes are best baked in a conventional gas or electric oven, rather than in a fan oven.

Don't open the oven door for the first 2 hours and always shut it very gently or the cake may drop. Ovens vary a great deal and if the cake seems to be browning too quickly lay a sheet of baking parchment across the top of the projecting lining paper, and reduce the heat to 140C / 275F / Gas mark 1 for the last half hour or so of baking time. Test with a warm metal skewer thrust several times around the centre of the cake, if it comes out clean of crumbs the cake is done.

Remove from the oven, leave in the tin for about 30 minutes before turning out onto a wire rack. When cold, wrap in greaseproof paper with lining paper still in place. Keep in an airtight tin to mature until needed.

DARK CHOCOLATE CAKE

Gluten-free. I use Celtic Irish Fine Dark Chocolate bars. You have to use good quality chocolate for baking, high in cocoa solids.

250 g / 9 oz dark, bitter chocolate (cooking chocolate will not do)

150 g / 5 oz castor sugar

150 g / 5 oz butter (not margarine)

75 g / 3 oz ground almonds

5 eggs

1 tbsp brandy (optional)

Melt the chocolate, sugar and butter gently in a bowl over a pan of simmering water. Once melted, stir thoroughly and add ground almonds. Separate the eggs. Beat the egg yolks one by one into the chocolate mixture. Beat the egg whites till stiff, stir in a large spoonful of the chocolate mixture before folding the egg whites into the rest of chocolate mixture very gently. Stir in the brandy if using at this point. Pour into a buttered and floured 8 inch / 20 cm cake tin.

Bake in a preheated oven, 180C / 350F / Gas mark 4 for 40 to 50 minutes. Leave in the tin till cold. Turn out on to a decorative plate, dust the top with icing sugar and serve with whipped cream.

CINNAMON APPLE CAKE

110 g / 4 oz soft margarine
110 g / 4 oz castor sugar
110 g / 4 oz self-raising flour
2 large eggs
A few drops vanilla essence

For the topping:

1 level tbsp castor sugar
2 level tsp powdered cinnamon
50 g / 2 oz flaked almonds
1 large cooking apple
Icing sugar for dusting

Use the all-in-one method of mixing – sift the flour into a bowl, add the margarine, sugar, eggs and vanilla essence and beat vigorously with an electric hand mixer for two or three minutes until well mixed. Turn the mixture into an eight-inch round cake tin, greased and lined on sides and bottom with greaseproof paper and leave the top open. Lightly mix the sugar, cinnamon and flaked almonds.

Peel, core and slice the apple very thinly and arrange the slices in an even layer on top of the cake mixture, then scatter the nut mixture evenly over the apple. Bake in the centre of a very moderate oven 180C / 350F / Gas mark 4 for about 30 minutes, or a little longer.

When done, remove from the oven, allow to cool slightly in the tin, then turn out into a plate covered with greaseproof paper lightly dusted with castor sugar. Invert onto a wire rack, so the apple topping is uppermost and leave to get cold, dust with icing sugar before serving. Delicious with mugs of hot cocoa.

COFFEE SANDWICH CAKE

110 g / 4 oz castor sugar

110 g / 4 oz butter

2 large eggs

2 tsp Irel coffee essence

110 g / 4 oz self-raising flour

4 tbsp raspberry jam, or make a little extra butter cream icing

For the butter cream icing:

110 g / 4 oz butter

225 g / 8 oz sifted icing sugar

2 tsp Irel coffee essence

Scant 2 tbsp warm water

25 g / 1 oz walnut halves for decoration.

Grease two 18 cm / 7 inch straight-sided sandwich tins, line bases with circles of non-stick Raytex paper. Beat the butter and sugar until light and fluffy, add the eggs one at a time, beating well after each addition and adding a light sprinkling of flour with the second one.

Beat in the coffee essence, then using a metal tablespoon fold in the sifted flour a little at a time. Divide the mixture evenly between the two tins and bake on the centre shelf of a preheated very moderate oven 180C / 350F / Gas mark 4 for about 25 minutes until done. Turn out onto a wire rack to cool.

To make the Coffee Butter Cream Icing: Remove the butter from the refrigerator well beforehand, cut into small pieces and cream until soft. Gradually beat in the sifted icing sugar, adding the Irel coffee essence. Beat well and if necessary add a little extra warm water to get a smooth creamy consistency. Spread the butter cream over the cake, pattern with the tines of a fork and decorate with walnut halves.

JUMBO-SIZED SWISS ROLL

Claire's recipe

Over-cooking toughens the surface and crisps the edges, spoiling the texture and making it difficult to roll up the sponge, so carefully time each swiss roll you bake until you know exactly how long it takes to get perfect results in your particular oven – make a note of the time that works best for you.

110 g / 4 oz castor sugar

4 large eggs

110 g / 4 oz plain flour

5 tsp warm water

Plus ingredients for the chosen filling

First line a swiss roll tin, 37x25 cm / 15x10 inches in size, with buttered grease-proof paper, or non-stick baking parchment. Stand the mixing bowl in a larger bowl containing hot water, break the eggs into it, add the sugar and leave to warm slightly. Meanwhile sift the flour twice. Then beat the eggs and sugar until fluffed up and much increased in volume – I give it at least 5 minutes with the hand-held electric mixer. The mixture should be very pale in colour and the beaters should leave a 'trail' for at least 5 seconds if drawn across the surface. Add the warm water, and beat thoroughly again.

Sift the already-sifted flour evenly on top of the mixture and use a metal table-spoon to fold it in – it can be quite tricky to get it mixed right through, so work gently to keep the texture light and full of air. Place a dab of the mixture in each corner of the lining paper to keep it in position.

Then quickly pour the mixture into the tin using a rubber scraper to clean round the mixing bowl. Instead of smoothing the surface with a knife, tilt the tin gently from side to side and end to end to get the mixture evenly distributed and en-sure that the corners fill evenly. Immediately place the tin on the shelf above the centre of a preheated hot oven 220C / 425F / Gas mark 7 and bake for about 10 to 12 minutes until nicely risen, golden, and springy to pressure with a finger.

When done, remove from the oven, loosen around the edges of the tin with a knife and turn out onto a clean tea towel lightly sprinkled with sugar. Carefully strip off the lining paper – it comes away easily if brushed with a pastry brush dipped in a little warm water. Trim away the crisp edge on the long sides, and if using plain jam as a filling, warm this in a small saucepan and spread it evenly over the still warm sponge, and roll it up immediately.

To get a neat cylindrical shape make a shallow cut on the outside about an inch in from one of the narrow ends so that this can be folded tightly inwards before starting to roll up, otherwise there will be a gap in the middle of each slice when you serve the swiss roll. Leave to cool.

If not using a jam filling, turn out, trim edges and make sure the inner short edge is tightly turned in, as above. Then roll up unfilled while still warm, keep wrapped in the teacloth until cold.

FRESH RASPBERRY AND CREAM FILLING

Mash about 225 g / 8 oz fresh ripe raspberries with sugar to taste, leave to stand for about 10 minutes then pour off excess juice. Unroll the sponge carefully, spread with a little softened butter to stop it getting too soggy.

Spoon the mashed raspberries over in an even layer, top with a layer of whipped cream, roll up again. Chill in the refrigerator for at least an hour before serving – delicious for a 'cream tea', or a special dessert!

Lemon or chocolate butter-cream icing, jam-and-whipped-cream, lemon curd with whipped cream and similar fillings are also put in after the swiss roll is cold, as above.

SMALLER VERSION – The above is a large and luxurious jumbo-sized swiss roll. For a scaled down version the ingredients are: 75 g / 3 oz castor sugar, 3 eggs, 75 g / 3 oz plain flour and 1 tablespoon warm water, and bake in a swiss roll tin measuring 30x23 cm / 12x9 inches at the same temperature as above for about 8 to 10 minutes.

JAM AND CREAM SPONGE

The same mixture given above for the smaller swiss roll (excluding the table-spoon of water and adding a pinch of salt) can be divided equally between 2 straight-sided 18 cm / 7 inch sandwich tins, previously buttered and dusted with flour.

Bake just above the centre of a moderate oven 190C / 375F / Gas mark 5 for about 15 minutes, until golden brown and springy to the touch. When done, turn out into a wire rack to cool, spread the base of both sponges with raspberry or strawberry jam, and sandwich together with whipped cream. Dust the top with castor sugar and chill before eating.

APPLE PIE

When we were at Careysville I made two or more apple pies a day throughout the harvest and the children used to carry them down to those working in the fields along with ham and jam sandwiches and gallons full of tea. If people were working late into the evening an extra food run was made which included bot-tled beer and lemonade.

    4 large cooking apples, peeled and sliced
    50 g / 2 oz sugar
    ¼ tsp ground cloves or cinnamon (optional)
    1 beaten egg yolk (optional)

Roll out half the pastry (given below) large enough to line the base of a Pyrex or enamelled plate that has already been lightly sprinkled with flour. Make sure the pastry lies flat against the base and trim off excess round the edges. Fill the centre of the plate up to 3 cm / 1 inch from the edge with the apple, making a nice domed shape towards the centre with the apple slices. If using, mix the spice into the sugar, then sprinkle the sugar over the apple.

Roll out the top of the pie. Dampen the edges of the pastry on the plate with a little water and place the topping over the filled pie plate. Trim the excess from the edges of the plate and seal the edges of the pie by crimping it gently. Using a pastry brush, paint the egg yolk in a thin layer over the surface of the pie, pierce the crust in several places and bake in a moderately hot oven 200C / 400F / Gas mark 6 for about 30 minutes. Remove from the oven when the crust is crisp and golden and has shrunk back from the edges of the pie plate. Serve with cream or custard and sugar to taste.

SHORTCRUST PASTRY

This takes about 20 minutes to make, and according to the old wives' tale cold hands and a warm heart make the best pastry! I prefer butter as it tastes good and gives a crisp finish.

250 g / 9 oz plain flour

A pinch of salt

125 g / 4½ oz butter, or half and half butter and white cooking fat, well-chilled beforehand

50 ml / 2 fl oz (10 tsp) ice cold water

Sift the flour and salt into a bowl. Cut the butter and fat into small pieces, add to the bowl and stir with the blade of a table knife until well coated. Working quickly and lightly rub the fat into the flour with your thumbs and fingertips, until it resembles fine bread crumbs, lifting your hands to let the mixture take up air as it drops back into the bowl as you go. Be careful not to over-mix. Add the water to the bowl all at once, and blend the mixture with the table knife until it comes together, adding a little extra water if it seems too dry. Turn out onto a lightly floured surface, gather together and shape quickly and lightly into a smooth ball with your hands. Leave to rest covered in a tea towel for 20 minutes in a cool place before using – this allows the gluten in the pastry to regain its elasticity.

MY WAY WITH MINCE PIES

Use ordinary shortcrust for the pastry shells – see previous recipe. Roll it out fairly thinly on a floured board and cut into circles (usually 6.5 cm / 2½ inches in diameter) to fit the patty tins. Cover with a clean tea towel and leave to rest for about 15 minutes – this helps to prevent the pastry shrinking while in the oven. Use shop bought frozen puff pastry for the lids. Roll out the pastry as given on the packaging and cut out the required number of smaller circles (usually 2 inches in diameter) which should be just large enough to lie across the top edges of the shortcrust shells.

Cover and leave to rest as above. For the filling use home-made mincemeat if possible, if using shop bought stir in about 4 tablespoons grated apple to each jar. Put a teaspoonful into each shell – do not be tempted to put in more at this stage. Brush the underside of each lid with beaten egg and place gently over the filling. Do not press the edges together, simply make a small slit in the centre of each with the point of a small kitchen knife to let the steam out and brush the top lightly with beaten egg.

Bake the trays of mince pies in a moderately hot oven 200C / 400F / Gas mark 6 for about 20 minutes or longer until the lids are nicely puffed up and golden brown and the pastry shells are cooked through. Ovens vary a good bit so make a note of the exact time they take in your oven for future reference. While the pies are baking, simmer some extra mincemeat with a dash of sherry or apple juice in a small saucepan for about 10 minutes, stirring all the time and making sure that all the suet is thoroughly melted in. Remove the pies from the oven when done, transfer rapidly to a wire rack and use a knife blade to raise the lid of each in turn just sufficiently to pop in a heaped teaspoon of cooked mincemeat, then press lightly back into position. This sounds complicated but it is very easy when you've got the hang of it, two pairs of hands are quicker (one pair to lift, the other to fill) and the results are truly delicious.

Store the mince pies in an airtight tin for up to a week, to be reheated as re-quired. Serve with whipped cream or fromage frais. According to superstition it's a good idea to eat twelve mince pies over the twelve days of Christmas to ensure twelve happy months the following year.

CHERRY CHOCOLATE DOT CAKE

This is an unexpected combination of ingredients but it's simple to make, turns out well and is very popular in our house because the walnuts, cherries and chocolate dots sink into a scrumptious sticky layer at the bottom.

225 g / 8 oz butter (preferable to margarine)

225 g / 8 oz castor sugar

4 large eggs

225 g / 8 oz plain flour sifted with 1½ level tsp baking powder

1 tablespoons warmish water

50 g / 2 oz glace cherries cut in half and sprinkled lightly with flour

50 g / 2 oz roughly chopped walnuts

50 g / 2 oz chocolate dots (bought in little packets)

A little extra castor sugar for dredging over the top or, if preferred,

a layer of pink glace icing decorated with halved cherries and walnuts

and chocolate dots.

Cream the butter and sugar until fluffy, then beat the eggs in one at a time with a sprinkling of flour after each one. Fold in the remaining flour adding a tablespoon or so of tepid water if the mixture is getting too stiff. Fold in the prepared walnuts, cherries and chocolate dots.

Turn the mixture into an oblong cake tin measuring 25 x 10 cm / 9 x 4 inches, previously greased and lined. Make a slight hollow in the centre to allow for rising, dredge the top with about a dessertspoon of granulated sugar if it's not going to be iced. Bake on the centre shelf of a very moderate oven 180C / 350F / Gas mark 4 for about 1½ hours, test with a warmed skewer thrust in 3 or 4 places which should come out clean of crumbs. Allow to cool in the tin for about 20 minutes, turn out onto a wire rack and immediately turn right-side up, leave to get cold before putting on the icing if using.

This cake is best eaten within about 3 days if it lasts that long, but it can be baked ahead, wrapped in foil and put in a polythene bag when cold and kept in the freezer until needed.

LUCY McCARTHY'S MARMALADE BRACK

This brack is so popular that Lucy McCarthy's special family recipe is requested over and over again by readers of my column in the *Irish Examiner*, and year after year she herself baked three dozen for the teas on our garden open days for charity!

400 g / 14 oz self-raising flour
350 g / 12 oz mixed dried fruit
1 level tsp mixed spice
1 well-rounded dessertsp marmalade
1 egg (standard size 2)
225 g / 8 oz brown sugar
300 ml / ½ pint hot strong tea

Have ready 2 loaf tins measuring 10 x 25 cm / 9 x 4 inches at the rim, rubbed with butter or margarine inside and then sprinkled lightly with flour. Pin a layer of brown paper around the outside. Put the dried fruit into a mixing bowl and pour in the hot tea. Cover with a tea towel and leave to steep overnight. Then add the marmalade and sugar, mix well and stir in the beaten egg. Using a metal table-spoon, fold in the flour, sifted with the mixed spice, and mix thoroughly. Divide the mixture equally between the two tins, cover each with butterpaper and bake in a preheated very moderate oven, 180C / 350F / Gas mark 4 for 1¼ hours.

Lucy tells me that at this stage she removes the butterpaper and has ready a scant dessertspoon of marmalade mixed with a teaspoon of hot water. She uses a pastry brush to spread the marmalade mix lightly over the top of each, then gives the bracks 10 minutes longer in the oven – that's what gives the gloss on top!

Having tested for doneness with a warmed skewer thrust into the centre, she turns the bracks out onto a wire rack as soon as they come out of the oven, inverts them on to another wire rack so that they face upwards, and covers them loosely with a tea towel to keep in the steam while they cool.

'My mother used to say that a brack should be moist inside, soft rather than crusty outside and sticky on top, so covering them like this gives the perfect finishing touch' said Lucy. These bracks also freeze perfectly and I keep two or three on hand, a great standby when friends or family drop by with very little warning!'

LINCOLN GINGER BISCUITS

(Makes about 36 biscuits)

225 g / 8 oz plain flour

Pinch salt

2 tsp ground ginger

225 g / 8 oz brown sugar

110 g / 4 oz butter

1 large egg

1 level tsp bread soda

1 tbsp milk

Blanched almonds or halved cherries for decoration

Sift the flour, salt and ginger into a bowl. Cut the butter into chunks and rub lightly into the flour mixture until the consistency is like fine breadcrumbs. Dissolve the bread soda in the milk and pour into the dry mixture along with the beaten egg, stir thoroughly. Turn onto a floured work surface and knead lightly and quickly into a smooth dough. Lightly damp the palms of your hands and form into round balls about the size of a walnut, place fairly far apart on greased baking sheets as these biscuits spread out during cooking, flatten slightly with the thumb and top each with a split almond or halved cherry.

Bake for about 30 minutes in a preheated low oven 170C / 325F / Gas mark 3, rotating the baking sheets so that the biscuits cook evenly. Use a palette knife to transfer onto a wire rack and leave to get cold and crisp.

Variations: Instead of ground ginger, use either 2 tsp of cinnamon, or ½ tsp nutmeg and 1 tsp mixed spice.

BUTTERSCOTCH BROWNIES

Teenagers enjoy making these and eat them immediately.

    50 g / 2 oz butter (not margarine)
    110 g / 4 oz soft brown sugar
    1 egg
    1 tsp vanilla essence
    50 g / 2 oz plain flour sifted with 1 tsp baking powder and ½ tsp salt
    50 g / 2 oz finely chopped walnuts.

Melt the butter and sugar in a small saucepan. Cool a little then beat in the egg and vanilla. Stir in the sifted flour and the chopped nuts, and then pour the batter into a shallow cake tin approx 8 inches square, previously greased and lined on the base. Bake for 20 to 25 minutes at 180C / 350F / Gas mark 4, and when cold cut into narrow fingers, lift out with a palette knife – a family favourite in our house.

FRUITY MACAROONS – gluten free

    2 egg whites
    110 g / 4 oz icing sugar
    110 g / 4 oz ground almonds or ground hazelnuts
    110 g / 4 oz dried fruit (your choice – cherries, mango, sultanas etc)
    Pinch of cinnamon

Chop the dried fruit finely. Make the meringue mix, whipping the egg whites until stiff, then beating in the icing sugar a spoonful at a time. Gradually add the other ingredients, stirring lightly with a metal spoon to keep the air in. Using 2 tsp, scoop the mixture into small mounds on a baking tray covered in greaseproof paper. Bake in a preheated oven, 150C / 300F / Gas mark 2, for 35 – 40 minutes till they spread and dry out. Serve these soft chewy biscuits when cold. Very good with hot strong coffee.

STICKY COCONUT MACAROONS – gluten free

4 egg whites
250 g / 9 oz castor sugar
250 g / 9 oz grated coconut
4 drops vanilla essence
Pinch of salt

Make the meringue mix as above. Gradually add the other ingredients, stirring lightly with a metal spoon to keep the air in. Using 2 teaspoons, scoop the mixture into small mounds on a baking tray covered in greaseproof paper. Bake in a preheated oven, 150C / 300F / Gas mark 2, for 35 – 40 minutes till they spread and dry out.

WHITE SCONES

Everybody loves scones with butter, red-berry jam and whipped cream for tea.

225 / 8 oz plain flour
Pinch of salt
1 level tsp bread soda
2 level tsp Bextartar
40 g / 1½ oz butter
40 g / 1½ oz castor sugar
150 ml / ¼ pint milk.

In a large mixing bowl sift together the flour, salt, bread soda and Bextartar. Working very lightly with your fingertips rub in the butter until the mixture resembles fine breadcrumbs, add the sugar, lightly mixing through your fingers until well mixed in. Pour the egg / milk mixture into a well in the centre of the dry mixture in the bowl and use a knife blade to mix quickly into a soft but not sticky dough.

Turn out onto a lightly floured surface, form lightly into a ball with your hands and pat or roll out to just over 1 cm / ½ inch thick. Stamp out the scones with a 5 cm / 2 inch scone cutter, pressing it straight down to prevent the sides of the scones rising unevenly. You should get about 9 to 12 scones if you gather up the trimmings to be rolled out again.

Put the scones on a floured baking tray and dust them lightly with flour too. Place near the top of a preheated hot oven 220C / 425F / Gas mark 7 and bake for about 10 minutes until risen and nicely browned. If not using at once place on a wire rack to cool and reheat when required.

Scones can be kept in a polythene bag in the freezer to be taken out as needed. Leave to defrost, then brush the top of the scones with a pastry brush dipped into milk and shaken before applying before heating up in a medium oven.

POTATO SCONES (TRADITIONAL)

Very good comfort food for everyone, even Taoiseachs, so I hear.

75 g / 3 oz plain flour

½ tsp baking powder

225 g / 8 oz smoothly mashed potatoes

A good pinch of salt

25 g / 1 oz butter

1 tbsp milk

Sift the flour, baking powder and salt into a bowl, rub in the butter until the mixture is like fine breadcrumbs and then mix in the mashed potatoes and milk to get a soft dough. Pat out gently on a floured surface, into a round about 1.5 cm / ½ inch thick, and cut into rounds about 4 cm / 1½ inches in diameter. Place on a baking sheet, brush the tops with milk or beaten egg, and bake in a hot oven 220C / 425F / Gas mark 7, for 15 to 20 minutes. Serve piping hot, to be split in half and buttered.

The same mixture can be used for delicious potato cakes. Simply pat, or roll the dough out about 1 cm / ¼ inch thick, cut into rounds with a scone cutter, and cook a few at a time on a well-greased griddle, or heavy frying pan. Turn when golden brown underneath and serve hot, again with butter!

CANADA JACK

A favourite in our offsprings' lunch boxes when they went to school; they made them themselves as teenagers.

175 g / 6 oz butter or margarine (or use half-and-half)
175 g / 6 oz brown sugar
225 g / 8 oz rolled oats
A good pinch of salt

Cream the butter and / or margarine in a bowl until light and fluffy. Add the sugar, rolled oats and salt and mix together very thoroughly. Butter a shallow rectangular tin measuring about 20x30 cm / 8x12 inches, spoon the mixture into it and smooth into an even layer.

Bake for 25 minutes in the centre of a moderately hot oven, 200C / 400F / Gas mark 6 until golden brown. Allow to cool slightly before cutting into 16 squares, then leave in the tin to get cold. Lift out carefully with a palette knife and keep in a tin until needed.

Buttermilk

Buttermilk is a traditional Irish dairy product used for drinking and making soda bread from times immemorial when cottagers with one cow made their own butter. The good news is that authentic butter milk is now being marketed in SuperValu by Cuinneogh who make Irish country butter. Healthy and nourishing it has the authentic flavour which everyone over about 55 grew up with – slightly fizzy, sourish with a tingling feeling on your tongue and a thickish texture. Many people believe it enhances the flavour of soda bread.

TRADITIONAL BROWN SODA BREAD

350 g / 12 oz coarse brown flour

110 g / 4 oz plain white flour

1 level tsp bread soda (bicarbonate of soda)

2 level tsp Bextartar

1 level tsp salt

Approximately 300 ml / ½ pint buttermilk or milk

Preheat the oven to moderately hot 200C / 400F / Gas mark 6. Have a greased baking tray ready. Measure out ½ pint of buttermilk or milk with about 3 table-spoons extra to hand. Weigh the brown flour and place in a mixing bowl. Weigh the white flour separately, add bread soda, Bextartar and salt, sift through a sieve into a bowl with the brown flour and run lightly through your fingers until well mixed. Pour in the measured buttermilk or milk all in one go and stir briskly with the blade of a knife until you have a moist but not sloppy dough.

Flour varies in the amount of liquid it takes up and if there are still traces of dry flour at the bottom of the bowl add a little more buttermilk or milk exactly where it's needed and mix quickly again – once you've had a bit of practice the whole process only takes 5 minutes. Turn the dough onto the greased baking tray, and use the knife blade to shape it quickly and lightly into a flattish round about 6 inches in diameter and 1½ inches thick – the 'cake' will be larger and higher if made with a double mix.

Make two deep slashes running from side to side in the form of a cross on top with a floured knife – this assists in the rising process – and place the baking sheet in the centre of the preheated oven without delay.

Bake for about 45 to 50 minutes (allow about 10 minutes more for the double mix) until well risen and nicely browned. Run a palette knife underneath just in case it is sticking to the baking tray anywhere, turn it over and test for 'doneness' by tapping the base with the knuckles to see if it sounds hollow, just as generations of Irish women have always done.

Leave it uncovered on a wire rack to cool and allow it to settle further for a couple of hours because soda bread is apt to crumble if cut too soon after it comes out of the oven. In our family we like a crunchy crust (which incidentally is better for healthy gums) but if you prefer a soft crust, wrap the 'cake' in a slightly damp tea towel until cold.

Topical Tips: too much bread soda will spoil the taste and the smell of your lovely home-made 'cake' as well as giving it a yellowish tinge, so be sure to use a 5 ml tsp. Vary the basic recipe to suit the family's taste – you could use 400 g /14 oz brown flour to 50 g / 2 oz white or substitute 50 g / 2 oz porridge oats for 50 g / 2 oz brown flour, while a dessertsp of black treacle gives a distinctive flavour.

WHITE SODA BREAD (TRADITIONAL)

900 g / 2 lb plain flour
1 tsp bread soda (bicarbonate of soda)
2 tsp cream of tartar (Bextartar)
600 ml / 1 pint buttermilk or milk
1 tsp salt

Sieve the flour, soda, cream of tartar and salt into a mixing bowl. Pour the buttermilk or milk into a well in the centre of the mixture, and stir briskly with the blade of a knife until most of the flour is taken up. Now knead lightly with floured hands, adding more milk if necessary – the dough should be rather soft. Shape the dough into a round flatish cake, about 22 cm / 9 inches across and place on a floured baking tin. Cut a cross on top to allow for rising and bake in moderately hot oven at 200C / 400F / Gas mark 6 for an hour or more, covering with foil about halfway through cooking time so that it does not get too brown.

RAISIN BREAD

The same as White Soda Bread, but, add one tablespoon of sugar and 175 g / 6 oz raisins to the flour before mixing in the milk.

MARY SCANLON'S LUXURY BROWN SODA BREAD

This is an extra special recipe from Mary Scanlon who with her husband John runs a Bord Fáilte Approved, Family Homes of Ireland guest-house in Conna, County Cork. Mary bakes her version of brown soda bread in a round 24 cm / 9½ inch diameter ovenglass casserole with a lid, which (like the bastable in the old days) keeps in the steam and produces a well-risen 'brown cake' with a soft crust, although very much richer in flavour and texture.

'Over the years I've adapted a very old recipe I originally got from Eily Brown of Strawhall, Fermoy who used to mind us when we were little – she was a great cook who had lovely recipes at a time when nobody else had them', Mary told me.

600 ml / 1 pint carton buttermilk

400 g / 14 oz Hearts Delight Wheatmeal flour

225 g / 8 oz Odlums Strong White flour

Pinch of salt

1 heaped tsp each of bread soda and Bextarter

Fistful of wheatgerm

50 g / 2 oz dark brown sugar (or to taste, I myself use 2 heaped tsp)

1 large egg

110 g / 4 oz butter (don't use margarine instead).

Put the wheatmeal into a large mixing bowl. Measure the strong white flour into a sieve with the salt, bread soda and Bextarter and sift into the bowl. Then add the wheat germ, brown sugar to taste (see above) and the butter cut into small pieces. Blend the mixture gently together using a pastry cutter or by making fast slashing strokes with a knife to break the butter into small fragments into the dry mixture. Then with hands held high run the mixture through your fingers (cold hands are a must, Mary says) to make sure everything is well mixed.

Make a well in the centre of the mixture, add the beaten egg to the buttermilk and pour in. Working quickly and lightly gather the mixture from the sides with one hand, turning the bowl as you go, until all the flour is wet. Still working lightly and rapidly turn the dough over on to itself again and again until it comes together into a wettish ball. Lay this into the well-buttered casserole without smoothing the surface out to the edges of the dish, and put on the lid.

Place the casserole immediately on the centre shelf of a preheated oven 200C / 400 F / Gas mark 6 and bake for 1 hour and 10 minutes – it always seems to take exactly that time. Mary swears by her wonderful Aga oven and tells me she never bakes it in a fan oven.

NO-KNEAD BROWN YEAST BREAD

This time-saving and easy to freeze bread recipe was devised by my daughter Claire. There is no kneading at all.

> 2 kg / 5 lb Howards' Wholemeal Stoneground brown flour
>
> 110 g / 4 oz / fresh baker's yeast (or failing this 2 sachets instant dried yeast following manufacturer's instructions)
>
> 4 tsp black treacle, honey or sugar
>
> 3 tsp salt
>
> 425 ml / ¾ pint warm water
>
> 1.2 litre / 2 pints hot water

Pour the flour into a large mixing bowl, add salt and run lightly through your fingers to mix. Break the yeast into chunky fragments, put into a bowl with the sweetener – treacle, honey or sugar – and dissolve in ¾ pint luke warm water. Leave in a warm place for 15 minutes or so until all bubbly and frothy, and in the meantime butter four 500 g / 1 lb loaf tins.

Make a well in the centre of the brown flour, pour in the frothing yeast and mix well. Add 1.2 litre / 2 pints of hot water, mixing quickly with a wooden spoon so as not to over-heat the yeast but to get a soft, wettish lukewarm dough without delay. Stir well and slash a cross over the top of the mixture – the dough starts rising immediately and marking it out into quarters like this before it puffs up ensures that an equal quantity goes into each of the four loaf tins. Spoon into the tins one by one then smooth over the top of each in turn, thoroughly wetting your hands under the tap each time – this assists rising and prevents cracking during baking as the wet surface doesn't skin over.

Leave to rise until the rounded tops are just above the rim of the tins – as you've started with luke warm dough this usually takes about 15 minutes, perhaps a little longer in cold weather. Bake in a hot oven 220C / 425F / Gas mark 7 for 40 to 50 minutes, switching the tins around about halfway through – the loaves are done when they have cooked slightly away from the sides of the tins, and sound hollow when tapped underneath with the knuckles.

To Freeze: leave loaves on a wire rack until completely cold, put each into a polythene bag fastened at the neck before freezing. Allow to thaw for about 3 hours at room temperature before slicing.

Variations: Claire leaves two of the loaves plain at each baking and flavours the other two in different ways by mixing any of the following into the dough for each loaf before it goes into the tins; 3 tablespoons of sunflower seeds per loaf, or 3 tablespoons coarsely chopped dates and / or 3 tablespoons chopped walnuts per loaf, or 2 tablespoons sultanas and 2 tablespoons poppy seeds per loaf look and taste unusual.

Topical Tip: extra supplies of fresh baker's yeast can be bought to be stored for up to a fortnight in a polythene bag in the refrigerator.

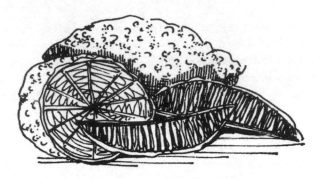

HOME-MADE JAMS AND PRESERVES

I think we must all have something of the squirrel instinct in us because it's very satisfying to lay in a store of home-made jams, jellies, chutneys and other preserves for year-round family use and to give away as presents.

I myself started, as people often do, using my largest saucepan. However I soon learned that a large preserving pan with heavy base is a necessity because, to get a good set when making jam, space is needed for a high rolling boil after the sugar has been added, and it's also very useful a when making chutney as bigger boilings can be made, a saving of time and fuel costs. All the following jam recipes, unless otherwise stated, yield about 4.5 kg / 10 lb.

A batch at a time: nowadays, with central heating and lack of cool storage places home-made jam, jelly and marmalade grow a greyish mould, or shrink and harden on top after relatively short time. So rather than making any of these in quantity it works well to make only one batch at a time, and freeze the required weight of berry fruits needed for several other batches in plastic bags to be used as needed throughout the year.

I always lightly butter the bottom and sides of the preserving pan before putting the fruit in to boil.

The following methods for testing for setting point; potting; covering, the jars and storage are the same for all jams unless otherwise mentioned.

Method of testing for setting point

Draw the jam / jelly off the heat, drop a scant teaspoonful on to a cold plate, leave for a couple of minutes then push against the blob of jam with the tip of a finger – if the surface wrinkles, you have a set. If it doesn't, return the preserving pan to high heat and boil hard for 3 minutes and test again, repeat testing once or twice at 3 minute intervals if required. When setting point is reached remove the pan from the cooker.

Method of potting jam

The empty jam jars must be cleaned, dried in a cool oven for about 20 minutes, then kept warm in a very low oven. Using a heat-proof jug pour jam / jelly into warm, dry jam jars, filling them right up to the neck, cover immediately with waxed discs and to avoid mould leave until completely cold before putting on the cellophane topping. Do not move the jars until the contents have set.

Successful storage: A cool, dark well-ventilated place is essential – an old-fashioned larder is ideal! Use up within a reasonable time to enjoy these preserves at their best.

BLACKCURRANT JAM

This is one of the easiest of all jams to make as the berries are high in pectin, the natural setting agent. It is best to pick the berries while they are still firm and not overripe, and if you have a freezer, strip from the stalks with a fork, freeze in 1.8 kg / 4 lb packs, to be made into jam as required.

   1.8 kg / 4 lb blackcurrants
   2.7 kg / 6 lb sugar
   1.8 litre / 3 pints water

Place the berries (freshly picked or defrosted if previously frozen) into a large heavy-based preserving pan. Add the water and simmer gently for about 30 minutes until a berry disintegrates when squeezed between thumb and forefinger. Add the sugar and stir until completely dissolved, boil hard for about 10 minutes then test for setting point, pot up into the jars, and cover and store as given above.

BLACKBERRY AND APPLE JAM

(Yield about 4.5 kg / 10 lb)

This sets easily and is simple to make. It isn't as pippy as jam made with blackberries alone and the unusual texture and flavour is very popular with children and grown-ups alike.

1.8 kg / 4 lb blackberries
700 g / 1½ lb apples
300 ml / ½ pint water
2.7 kg / 6 lb sugar
Juice of a lemon

Place the blackberries (defrost first if previously frozen) in a pan with a quarter pint of water, and the apples previously peeled and cored in another pan with the remaining ¼ pint of water. Simmer both gently over a low heat until soft and broken down to a pulp, mash well.

Combine the two in a large preserving pan, bring back to the boil, add the juice of a lemon and all the sugar, then stir well until the sugar has completely dissolved. Turn up the heat and boil fast, setting point is usually reached in about 15 minutes, so start testing after 12 minutes; pot up into the jars, cover and store as given above.

GREEN GOOSEBERRY JAM

(Yield about 4.5 kg / 10 lb)

Gooseberries are also high in pectin which is needed for a good set so this is another very good jam for beginners. The best gooseberry jam is made from slightly unripe berries because the skins get tougher and the pips darken as the berries ripen, spoiling the appearance, flavour and texture of the jam.

Well-made green gooseberry jam is an attractive greeny-golden colour.

2 kg / 4½ lb gooseberries
2.7 kg / 6 lb sugar
900 ml / 1½ pints water
About 2 tsp butter, which helps prevent frothiness

Use smaller quantities if not using a full-size preserving pan as there must be space for a high rolling boil after the sugar has been added –

1.35 kg / 3 lb gooseberries
1.8 kg / 4 lb sugar
600 ml / 1 pint water
Knob of butter

Wash the gooseberries to remove any spray, then top and tail them (i.e. remove the stalk and tiny brown tuft at the flower end), and make a small nick in the skin with a sharp knife – this speeds up the softening process, especially if you're using fruit which is on the ripe side.

Butter the base and sides of a large preserving pan, put in the gooseberries with the water and simmer gently for about 30 minutes over low heat without the lid, until the berries are breaking down to a pulp – remember to stir now and then to prevent the fruit catching on the bottom.

At this stage I always use an old-fashioned potato masher to break up the berries and get rid of any white froth trapped under the skin. Add the sugar, then stir briskly with a wooden spoon until it is completely dissolved, with no grittiness left. Raise the heat and bring to a fast boil until setting point is reached, start testing after about 12 minutes as described above.

Remove from heat – at this point, instead of skimming off the whitish foam I add 2 teaspoons butter and stir like mad until all the frothiness has been absorbed back into the jam without a trace. Pot up and store jam in a cool, well-ventilated place.

Variations: (1) For Gooseberry and Orange Jam use 150 ml / ¼ pint less water and add 150 ml / ¼ pint freshly-squeezed orange juice and the finely grated rind of 2 well-scrubbed oranges; (2) for a subtle muscatel grape flavour, briefly swish 2 or 3 freshly picked heads of elderberry flowers around in the fruit pulp just before adding the sugar, discard after use.

FREEZER STRAWBERRY CONSERVE

I obtained this recipe from Elizabeth Corban Lucas, a keen grow-your-own gardener who believes in stowing away the fruits of the earth to be enjoyed year round! Raspberries and loganberries are equally good.

550 g / 1¼ lb strawberries

900 g / 2 lb castor sugar

2 tbsp lemon juice

150 ml / ¼ pint bottled pectin (Certo)

Crush the strawberries – a potato masher is ideal – in a bowl. Add the sugar and lemon juice and leave for about an hour stirring occasionally until the sugar has dissolved. Add the liquid pectin and stir vigorously for 2 minutes until thoroughly mixed. Pour into small containers for the freezer – empty crème fraiche or cottage cheese tubs with lids are ideal – leaving 1 cm space from the top to allow for expansion. Leave in a cool place to set for 24 hours. Put on the lids, seal the containers, and freeze. Keep upright in the freezer as the jam is not solid so may ooze.

This conserve thaws rapidly so can be used at short notice as jam or a sauce for ice cream. Tastes of fresh strawberries as the fruit is not cooked.

SEVILLE ORANGE MARMALADE

Marmalade is the first of the jam preserves for the year.

There's nothing like the delicious bitter tang of home-made Seville orange marmalade to get the day off to a good start. This is far more authentic in flavour than some commercial kinds, particularly those that have a high sugar content and / or the peel is often conspicuous by its absence.

January is the start of the marmalade-making season, much looked forward to by those who enjoy making preserves of all kinds, the bitter oranges are in the shops for only a short season so don't delay. Choose firm well-coloured fruit, avoiding the green ones. Also Seville oranges tend to go bad if left too long. Many hands make light work and if you're purchasing a fair amount get the family to give a hand with cutting up the peel.

Rather than making marmalade in quantity at the start of the season it is best to make only one batch of 10 jars for immediate use and make subsequent batches as needed. This is easily done if you prepare several measured batches of cut peel up to the point where sugar would normally be added. Ladle each batch into a large polythene bag, tie tightly at the neck leaving room for expansion as it freezes, and store in the freezer to be freshly made at intervals as required throughout the year.

1.35 kg / 3 lb Seville oranges

3 large lemons

3.6 litres / 6 pints water

2.7 kg / 6 lb sugar

A knob of butter the size of a walnut.

The oranges and lemons must be carefully scrubbed to remove the protective spray. Take off the small green disc at the stalk end. Then cut the fruit in half across the segments. Much of the pectin (setting agent) is in the pips and pith of the oranges and lemons so collect these in a small bowl as you go along. Use a lemon squeezer to press out the orange and lemon juice, strain through a sieve into the preserving pan and put the pips into a small bowl. Use the edge of a dessertspoon to scoop the tough membranes and pulp from the halved fruit and add this to the pips in the bowl, also cut away some of the thick white pith of the lemon halves with a sharp knife and add to the bowl.

While the slicing attachment on a food processor gives a quick result, the appearance of the finished marmalade is more appealing if the orange and lemon peel is cut by hand. The fineness of the cut peel is a matter of choice – a little on the thick side if you like your marmalade chunky or alternatively use a sharp knife to cut it into thin slivers – it's much quicker to do this if you cut the squeezed out skins in half first. Also it's better to do the boiling on the same day because the peel dries out if left overnight and soaking is not of benefit.

Put the cut peel into the preserving pan and add all the water. Tie the contents of the bowl into a 30 cm / 12 inch square of muslin, loosely enough for the water to extract the pectin by circulating through the pith and the pips during the preliminary boiling time, yet making sure that none of the pips will escape into the marmalade. Place the muslin bag in the preserving pan.

Citrus peel is tougher than the soft fruit and berries used for jam, so requires a longer boiling time. Bring the cut peel in the preserving pan slowly to the boil and continue to simmer gently over low heat without the lid, stirring now and then, for about 2 hours or a little longer, until the peel is soft when squeezed between forefinger and thumb and the volume of fruit pulp in the preserving pan has dropped considerably due to evaporation. Remove the muslin bag and squeeze hard so that the high pectin juice runs back into the pan.

NB: stop at this point if this is one of the batches being prepared for use later in the year, in which case the contents of the preserving pan must be left until completely cold, then poured into a large polythene bag and stored in the freezer until needed. When you want to use it, remove from the freezer, tear the polythene bag away from the frozen peel and leave to thaw in the preserving pan. Then bring to boiling point over low heat and proceed with the recipe as given below.

Still at low heat, add the sugar all in one go and stir briskly with a wooden spoon until completely dissolved – there should be no grittiness left at the bottom of the pan. Then turn up the heat to high, boil rapidly with the marmalade rising in the pan until setting point is reached, usually within about 15 to 20 minutes providing that the boiling has been fast enough – that's why it's so important to have a preserving pan!

To test for setting point draw the pan off the heat after 15 minutes, drop a scant teaspoonful of the marmalade onto a cold plate, leave to cool for a minute or so, push the edge of the blob with the tip of a finger, if it wrinkles you have a set. If not return the pan to high heat, boil hard for another 3 minutes and repeat the test, and repeat again if necessary. When you have a set, remove the preserving pan from the heat, drop in a knob of butter, and stir quickly and thoroughly until the white froth on the surface has been reabsorbed. Remove any remaining white blobs and allow the marmalade to cool for about 15 minutes before potting up – this helps to prevent the peel from rising in the jars.

Use a jug to pour the marmalade into warm dry jars right up to the neck. Wipe the rim of the jars with a damp cloth. Cover with waxed circles while still hot, and leave until cold before putting on the cellophane topping. Don't move the jars until the marmalade has set.

APPLE JELLY

Make the most of windfalls as slightly unripe apples give a good, sharp flavour and a strong easy set, and it's a good idea to lay in enough frozen apple juice to make batches of jelly year round. The same recipe is used for wild crab apples which have a very special flavour, if you don't have sufficient juice to make a batch top up with ordinary apple juice.

You can make your own jelly bag from strong cotton material about 86 cm / 34 inches square, fold into a triangle and machine stitch up one of the open sides to give a point through which the juice drips, alternatively set aside an old pillow case for this specific purpose, scald then fill with apple pulp and suspend over the bucket, making sure one of the one bottom corners is lower than the other so the juice drips out through it.

When making the juice you need apples, water to cover and added flavouring such as cloves, bruised whole ginger or lemon peel.

Wash the fruit, cut up into chunks, discarding any bad or bruised parts. Put into the preserving pan with just enough water to cover i.e. about 1.5 litres / 2½ pints water to 2 kg / 4½ lb chopped apples, along with the chosen flavouring, and simmer gently for about an hour or so until broken down to pulp.

Mash with a potato masher, scald the jelly bag in boiling water, then use a jug to transfer the fruit pulp into it and hang it up over a clean bucket to drip. It is essential to use the juice or pour it into bags to freeze within 24 hours.

It is always said that squeezing the bag results in cloudy jelly, but I have found that a good squeeze produces about a pint of extra juice, and simply strain this through a double thickness of coffee filter papers to get a lovely clear preserve.

To freeze the juice simply pour 600 ml / 1 pint into polythene bags, tie tightly at the top to prevent leakage and place it in a plastic pudding bowl for support in the freezer until frozen.

When making the jelly you need 2.25 kg / 5 lb sugar, 2.7 litres / 5 pints prepared juice, the juice of 2 lemons and 3 or 4 cloves if you like the flavour.

Measure the juice into your preserving pan, add the lemon juice and cloves if using, bring to the boil over medium heat. Add the sugar and keep stirring hard until all the sugar has dissolved completely. Then turn up the heat to get a high rolling boil until setting point is reached, usually within about 10 to 15 minutes.

After 10 minutes fast boiling the 'flake test' is used to check setting point. Remove the preserving pan from the heat, dip the wooden spoon into the pan and bring it out with a little of the jelly in the bowl of the spoon, allow a minute or so to get cold.

Then slowly keep turning the spoon held horizontally in your hand until the jelly reaches the edge. If it has been sufficiently boiled to set, instead of dripping off fairly fast the drops will run together and elongate into flakes which will break off sharply and cleanly. If you don't have a set return the preserving pan to high heat, boil fast for 3 minutes and test again – this may be repeated at 3 minute intervals until you have a set.

(This test may seem tricky at first but you will learn with experience – believe it or not I like to stand in an open doorway where there's a cool breeze to do this!)

Have warm dry jars set out ready for immediate filling. Jelly starts to set very quickly so skim the froth off as rapidly as possible with a large warm spoon, try to remove small traces by drawing a piece of newspaper with a torn edge across the surface as speedily as possible. Use a jug to pour quickly into the jars, holding each one tilted at an angle so that the jelly will run down the sides without trapping air bubbles. Place the waxed discs in position immediately. Leave until the jelly has set before covering with cellophane topping, store in a cool dark place.

HOME-MADE CHUTNEY
(Yield about 4.5 kg / 10 lb)

Chutneys of different kinds are delicious with cold beef, lamb, pork and chicken, a spoonful can make all the difference to the flavour of a sauce; adds interest to individual helpings of stew or savoury mince and relish to a ploughman's lunch of brown bread and cheese. The amount of sweetness and spiciness can be adjusted to suit family preferences so once you've got the hang of it, making your own chutney is a creative occupation, and ideal for beginners as very little can go wrong in the cooking!

There are a few general rules to be followed:

• long slow cooking from 1 ½ to 2 hours is needed to get the right consistency and allow the flavours to combine well,

• brown vinegar and brown sugar result in a rich, dark preserve while white vinegar and granulated sugar is used if a lighter colour is preferred,

• onions get tough if cooked in vinegar, so if using them in the recipe boil them in water until cooked through beforehand,

• chutney needs at least 2 months to mature before use, and would-you-believe keeps well in screw top jars for 2 to 3 years,

• for potting up you need empty mayonnaise, pickle, and chutney jars and / or instant coffee jars which have lacquered lids as vinegar corrodes unprotected metal so it's a very good idea to remind friends to keep collecting the appropriate jars and the lids for you.

APPLE AND SULTANA CHUTNEY

Windfalls are ideal for this provided they're not under-ripe and all the bruised parts are discarded, also you can use your own choice of spices to vary the flavour. Double quantities can be made if you have a large preserving pan!

NB: it is worth noting that onions don't soften well in vinegar so you need to chop them small and cook in water before you start the chutney-making.

1.35 kg / 3 lb cooking apples weighed after peeling and coring

900 g / 2 lb sultanas

225 g / 8 oz onions, chopped and cooked in boiling water till soft

1 dessertsp ground cinnamon

1 dessertsp ground ginger

1 tsp ground nutmeg

25 g / 1 oz salt

1.2 litre / 2 pints white vinegar

700 g / 1 ½ lb granulated sugar (or use brown if preferred).

Chop the apples fairly small after peeling and coring, place in a large heavy-bottomed saucepan or preserving pan with the sultanas, cooked and chopped onions, spices, salt, vinegar and sugar and stir well over gentle heat until the sugar has dissolved. Simmer without the lid for about 2 hours stirring frequently to prevent catching on the bottom – the chutney will be ready when the consistency is thick, smooth and pulpy.

Remove the pan from the heat and use a heat-proof jug to pour the chutney into warm dry jars, cover with screw-on lids as described above. Store until needed in a cool place.

GREEN AND RED PEPPER CHUTNEY

Devised by Val

900 g / 2 lb brown sugar

1.35 kg / 3 lb apples, peeled and chopped

450 g / 1 lb each red and green peppers, cut into chunks large enough to lend colour as well as flavour to the finished chutney

900 g / 2 lb sultanas

900 ml / 1 ½ pint white vinegar

1 tbsp salt

1 tbsp fresh ginger, peeled and chopped fairly small

2 tsp powdered cinnamon.

Method: as for Apple and Sultana Chutney.

PICKLED BEETROOT

This is one of the simplest and most popular of pickles.

Wash the beets, cut away the leaves leaving a tuft of stalks about an inch long, and be careful not to break the skin or snap off any of the rootlets because this allows the colour to leach out during boiling.

Place in a large saucepan of lightly salted water and simmer gently for about 1 ½ hours, if using a pressure cooker follows the manufacturer's instructions, usually 20 minutes at 15 lb pressure. Leave in the water until cold.

Strip off the skin, slice into rounds at least a third of an inch thick (if thinner than this the beetroot flavour is overpowered by the vinegar) and divide the slices into halves or quarters, depending on the size of the beets.

Pack into clean, dry jars, previously washed thoroughly, then left in a very low oven to dry and sterilise – empty pickle or mayonnaise jars with lacquered lids, or instant coffee jars with plastic lids are ideal as unprotected metal lids will be corroded by the vinegar during storage.

Boil up 1.2 litre / 2 pints vinegar (repeat this if you need more) – white is prefer-able to brown as it gives a better colour – adding 1 tsp salt and 1 or 2 tsp sugar to each pint, plus about 8 cloves, a few peppercorns and about a tsp of whole spice, if you like a spicy flavour. Simmer for about 5 minutes, strain through a sieve, then immediately pour the boiling vinegar over the prepared beetroot in the jars, covering the top slices by at least 1.5 cm / ½ inch, allow to cool, then wipe the neck of the jar and screw on the lid.

Stored in a cool dark place, such as a cold larder. This pickle keeps well for a year or longer.

JELLIED BEET

A favourite with many people, this has pleasant flavour and consistency and the juice doesn't drip onto the tablecloth, causing those unmistakable crimson stains.

Mix a packet of strawberry, blackcurrant or raspberry jelly with 425 ml / ¾ pint of water and vinegar, mixed half-and-half, then boiled up together, stir until dissolved. Pour over diced or sliced cooked beetroot in a glass dish for immediate use, or into small jars with screw-on lids for later use, and leave to set.

CUCUMBER AND ONION PICKLE

One of our family favourites, this pickle is easy to make and has a nice tang, good with cold meat, chicken or cheese, it also keeps well for many months.

    3 large cucumbers
    4 large onions
    4 level tbsp salt
    600 ml / 1 pint white vinegar
    175 g / 6 oz granulated sugar
    A few pepper corns
    A good pinch of culinary celery seed if liked

Wash and dry the cucumbers, cut into fairly thin slices and mix in a large bowl with the onions, also fairly thinly sliced. Sprinkle the salt over and leave for 2 hours to draw the juices, rinse in batches in a sieve under the cold tap and drain well.

Bring the vinegar, sugar and spices (if using) to the boil, simmer gently for 3 minutes. Meanwhile place the sliced cucumber and onion loosely into clean dry jars, a pound size are best. Pour in the hot vinegar to cover, use a skewer to dislodge any trapped air-bubbles, screw the lids on tightly and store in a cool, dark place until needed.

SPICED ORANGE RINGS
(Yields about 1.8 kg / 4 lb)

These are a real luxury, very unusual and they always cause comment, top favourite with the salmon anglers who greatly appreciated the wide selection of the home-made preserves I devised for the guests at Careysville.

　10 small thick skinned oranges

　600 ml / 1 pint white wine vinegar

　1.15 kg / 2½ lb cane or loaf sugar

　1½ stick cinnamon

　About 20 cloves

　1 tsp ground mace

　1.8 litre / 3 pints water

Scrub the oranges under a warm tap. Cut each orange into fairly thick rings (7 mm / ¼ inch), cutting through the segments from stem-end to blossom end. Lay the rings in a preserving pan, add the water and simmer with the lid on until the peel is tender. Remove from heat.

Make a syrup of the vinegar, sugar and spices in a large saucepan. Reserving the cooking water, remove half the orange rings from it and lay them in the syrup; make sure they are all covered. Put the lid on and simmer for 30 – 40 minutes till the orange peel turns clear, then remove them from the pan and place in a bowl. Simmer with the remaining orange rings in the syrup. Add the previously cooked slices to the pan, taking care to keep the rings whole. At this point, if there isn't enough syrup to cover all the orange rings make up the difference by gently stirring in some of the cooking water. Replace pan lid and leave the orange rings to steep overnight in the syrup.

Next day, remove orange rings and then thicken the syrup by boiling with the lid off the pan, allowing steam to escape. Return the orange rings to the pan, reheat it gently and then re-boil for a 8 – 10 minutes.

Lay the orange rings on top of each other in sterilised 1 lb screw-top jars and pour in the syrup covering over the upper-most ring and leave them to get cold. Screw the lids on and allow to mature for 6 weeks.

This preserve look and tastes terrific, is great with all sorts of cold meats, hot roast pork or roast duck and very sophisticated with a cheese board. Can be stored for months in a cool dark place.

THERE'S ALWAYS ROOM AT OUR HOUSE

Whether you are having a drinks party, a fork supper or a child's birthday tea, the secret is to plan ahead. Choose the menu carefully so that much of it can be prepared in advance and relax and enjoy the company, and never apologise for any small short-comings.

In this edition I have not given details of how to plan celebratory and festive meals. Many of the recipes in the book will double and even treble-up for more people and there's plenty to choose from. What I will say is that giving a party should be fun for the hosts as well as the guests.

There is no need to be competitive or over-generous with the food, cook things you are confident with. For large or informal events use disposable glasses and plates, not very environmentally correct perhaps, but just think of the washing up you'll save.

Spend plenty of time making your home and / or garden welcoming, make sure there are places where people can sit and chat, and others a bit out of hearing where people can play music or just be loud. Remember that people come to your parties to be with you and flourish in your company – so just relax and enjoy!

A DRINKS PARTY

Plan the 'eats' first. Nowadays, there are so many finger foods – crisps, tortillas with ready prepared dips in screw top jars, savoury biscuits, nuts, olives and so on available that I rarely cook the nibbles to go with drinks. I don't see this as a drop in standards because it leaves me with more time to be with my guests

WHAT TO DRINK

The choice of drinks is wide – anything from champagne, to sherry, cocktails, white of red wine, beer, mulled wine, 'Cup' or a selection including gin, whiskey, vodka and brandy. If anyone asks for a small drink, give him or her just that. Have soft drinks for those who prefer them: Ame, ginger beer, still and carbonated water, pineapple juice, Cidona, or tomato juice which can be pepped up with added salt and black pepper, lemon juice and a dash of Worcester sauce and chopped mint. Have ice cubes at hand to add at the last moment.

Mulled Wine

Good for a winter party, the following quantities serve 6 to 8 people (one wine glass each). One bottle of red wine such as Claret or Burgundy, the peel of an orange, ½ a lemon, a piece each of cinnamon and root ginger, two cloves, a pinch of mace, 110 g / 4 oz sugar. Boil the chopped orange peel, thinly sliced lemon, cinnamon, root ginger, cloves, mace and sugar in 300 ml / ½ pint water for five minutes, stirring constantly until the sugar melts. Add the red wine, stir and heat until nearly boiling, strain and serve hot.

White Wine Cup

Serves 8 to 10 (one wine glass each). One bottle of hock or other white wine, an equal quantity of soda water or lemonade (or a mixture of both) a few leaves of mint, thinly sliced lemon and ice. Add a wine glass of brandy if liked. Chill the wine and soda water or lemonade, mix together just before serving, pour into glasses with ice cubes, and garnish each with a slice of lemon and a mint leaf.

Red Wine Cup

Substitute the red for the white and proceed as for the White Wine Cup, but garnish with thinly sliced orange, the faintest taste of grated nutmeg and ice cubes.

HOME-MADE LEMONADE

350 g / 12 oz sugar

5 lemons

1.8 litre / 3 pints water

A few mint leaves

Pare the thoroughly washed lemon rinds thinly, simmer with the water, sugar and mint leaves for five minutes, stirring occasionally. Strain through a sieve, cool and then add the juice of the lemons, stir well and serve as cold as possible.

CHILDREN'S PARTIES

Children's parties often sound like an ordeal but they don't have to be – however you must always be alert and keep a watchful eye.

Prepare your house, put everything breakable out of the way and get rid of any clutter. Children enjoy themes – so perhaps get them to dress up, organise a treasure hunt in a local park or take them swimming. Wear them out before they eat!

As children tend to be naturally cautious there is no need to be wildly creative with what they eat. Plan the food around things that they know – crisps, small filled bread rolls, sausage rolls, dainty sandwiches, little iced sponge buns (page 140) or un-iced warm from the oven are hugely popular. Boxed juice drinks are convenient if you're away from home and don't forget that all children love balloons.

At any age, children love making their own puddings with ice cream – I like to use the Corrin Hill ice cream that's made in Fermoy and taste-tested on children. Supply bowls, spoons, ice creams in tubs – vanilla, sticky toffee and / or chocolate are the preferred flavours, fruit sauces, 100s and 1000s to sprinkle, and let them get on with it – but take charge if you need to.

THE LAST WORD

I once knew a young man – really a most pleasant and well-meaning young man – who, fresh from university, joined a small Irish firm. Within a month he was highly unpopular with the whole staff, most puzzling until I heard an old workman talking about him.

'Sometimes I have pity for him, and more times I haven't,' he said. 'There he is, waving his certificates in his hand, proud as a peacock and bursting with judgement.'

What a very apt and telling phrase, I do hope I have not given that impression! It is just that I believe good food is one of the pleasures and blessings of life. I enjoy cooking, eating, and talking about food. While revising this book I have discovered so many things that my family and readers have taught me, it's also been a trip down memory lane for the children. Writing it has given me immense pleasure, a renewed interest in my own kitchen and in effect it is a celebration of what I've learned about cooking since the day in June 1951 when my darling husband Val (who was very thin and scrawny after his experiences as a Japanese prisoner of war) told me with an impish smile that he didn't want to eat food because it was good for him, but because he liked what was on his plate.

That really made me think, we had 42 happy, happy years together, and I firmly believe that love and a determination to be a good cook is what good food is all about.

I will end as I began with a rather cynical quotation from Owen Meredith:

'He may live without books, – what is knowledge but grieving?
He may live without hope, – what is hope but deceiving?
He may live without love, – what is passion but pining?
But where is the man who can live without dining?'

INDEX